FRANK ZAPPA: guitar, octave bass, percussion.

CAPTAIN BEEFHEART

IAN UNDERWOOD: piano, organus maximus, flute, all clarinets, all saxes.

MUSICIANS: CAPTAIN BEEFHEART—vocal on "Willie The Pimp" (courtesy Straight Records) ☐ SUGAR CANE HARRIS—violin on "Willie The Pimp" & "The Gumbo Variations" ☐ JEAN LUC PONTY—violin on "It Must Be A Camel" (courtesy World Pacific Records) ☐ JOHN GUERIN-drums on "Willie The Pimp", "Little Umbrellas" & "It Must Be A Camel" ☐ PAUL HUMPHREY—drums on "Son Of Mr. Green Genes" & "The Gumbo Variations" ☐ RON SELICO—drums on "Peaches En Regalia" ☐ MAX BENNETT—bass on "Willie The Pimp", "Son Of Mr. Green Genes", "Little Umbrellas", "The Gumbo Variations" & "It Must Be A Camel" ☐ SHUGGY OTIS—bass on "Peaches En Regalia" ☐ ☐ ☐ *ENGINEERS:* DICK KUNC— Whitney Studios ☐ JACK HUNT—T.T.G. ☐ CLIFF GOLDSTEIN—T.T.G. ☐ BRIAN INGOLDSBY—Sunset Sound ☐ Recorded 16 track August through September 1969 ☐ ☐ Mastered 2008 by Bernie Grundman from FZ's original edited master. ☐ Art Direction & Concept by Frank Zappa, NT&B. ☐ Cover design: CAL SCHENKEL ☐ Cover Photos: ANDEE NATHANSON ☐ Interior design: JOHN WILLIAMS ☐ All Compositions composed & arranged by Frank Zappa, controlled worldwide by Munchkin Music. All rights reserved.

Zappa Alert: Andee Nathanson, the actual "Hot Rats" album cover photographer, wasn't properly credited for her iconic photograph until 2012.

SIDE ONE: 22:19

PEACHES EN REGALIA 3:58
WILLIE THE PIMP 9:25
SON OF MR. GREEN GENES 8:58

SIDE TWO: 21:22

LITTLE UMBRELLAS 3:09
THE GUMBO VARIATIONS 12:55
IT MUST BE A CAMEL 5:15

thanks forever miss christine.

"There's a recording that I picked up in Europe that had 'The Shadow of Your Smile' with Archie Shepp playing on it. He played this solo that just sounded to me immediately like there was this fucking army of pre-heated rats screaming out of his saxophone. That's what it sounded like. That's where I got the title of the *Hot Rats* album." — Frank Zappa

FRANK ZAPPA

HOT RATS

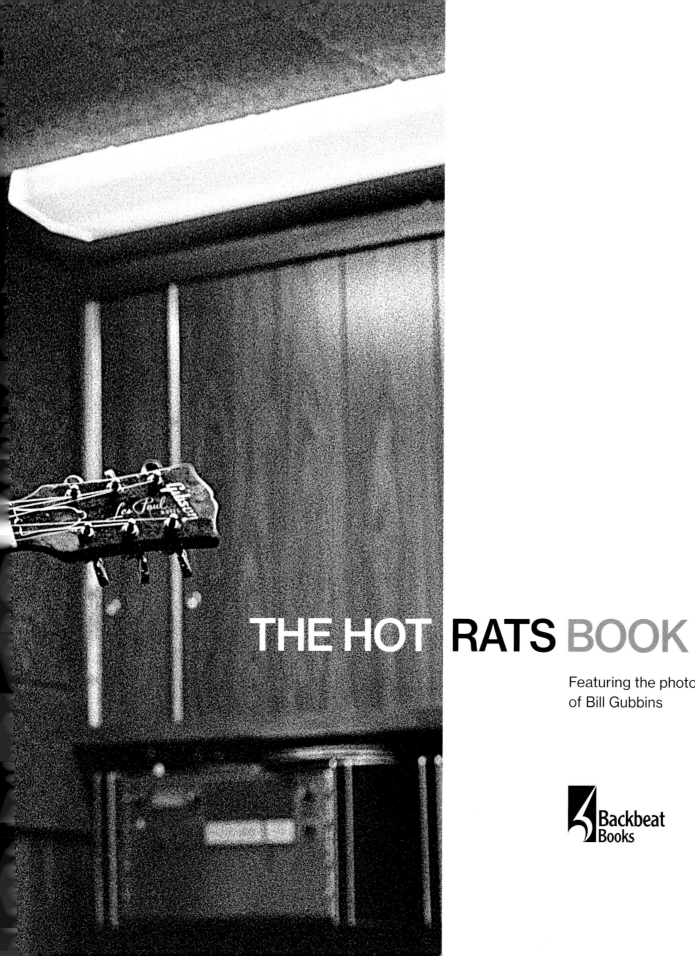

THE HOT RATS BOOK

Featuring the photographs
of Bill Gubbins

Backbeat
Books

Published by Backbeat Books
An imprint of The Rowman & Littlefield Publishing Group, Inc.
4501 Forbes Blvd., Ste. 200
Lanham, MD 20706
www.rowman.com

Distributed by NATIONAL BOOK NETWORK

Project Development Manager, Melanie Starks
Hot Rats album cover photographer, Andee Nathanson
Book Design by Mike Fink

Library of Congress Cataloging-in-Publication Data available

ISBN 978-1-4930-4775-8 (hardback)

The paper used in this publication meets the minimum requirements of American
National Standard for Information Sciences – Permanence of Paper for Printed Library
Materials, ANSI/NISO Z39.48-1992

Printed in the United States of America

CONTENTS

I read, listened and learned everything I could about this mustachioed wizard.

photo: Kendrick Brinson / New York Times / Redux

FOREWORD
BILLY BOB THORNTON

In June of 1966 when the album *Freak Out!* was released, I was just a month and a half short of my 11th birthday and riding my purple bicycle around Malvern, Arkansas in the dog days of summer with other nerdy kids who would actually talk to me. We all looked like Ernie Douglas from *My Three Sons*. And we were music freaks. Music and baseball were the only things that we thought about. We had one record store in town called Paula's Record Shop. Most of us couldn't afford to buy an album, but once in a while lawn mowing money provided enough to get a 45. The good news was that most households did have a record player, mostly cheap ones, but who cares? We weren't exactly audio engineers. As a result of this lack of dollars, we would go into Paula's and just flip through the albums looking at the pictures of the bands and reading whatever information was on the back cover. I was actually unable to contain myself on one occasion and peeled off the wrap on a double album to see what was inside. I was promptly escorted out by Paula, who was a no-nonsense kind of gal. When I first gazed upon the album *Freak Out!* and saw these scary looking guys called the Mothers of Invention and then flipped it over for my first taste of Suzy Creamcheese, I became obsessed before even hearing a note of the music. "How mysterious. I mean look at those guys. I want to be one of those guys." Then a guy moved to our town from the exotic state of Connecticut. AND HE HAD A COPY OF *FREAK OUT!* I badgered my way into his life and heard "Who Are the Brain Police?" "Wowie Zowie" and "Hungry Freaks, Daddy,"

with my own ear bones and my life was changed forever. I always knew there was something else out there. Somewhere, that humor and those different sounds existed. And my creepy little pals and I had found it. After that initial experience, then along came *Absolutely Free*, *We're Only In It For The Money*, *Cruising with Ruben & the Jets*, *Uncle Meat*, and a personal favorite, *Burnt Weeny Sandwich*. I became Zappa-ized forever. I read, listened and learned everything I could about this mustachioed wizard. One thing about fans of Frank Zappa, is that they all seemed to feel different growing up and outside the mainstream. Once they listened they felt like they belonged to some secret society they knew existed but was hard to find. I never got to meet him. I was just a couple of years late, but over the years I got to know and be accepted by his family, for which I am eternally grateful. I have bothered them for well over twenty years with questions about Frank. Now to the point—another kid whose life was changed by the mind and art of Zappa is Bill Gubbins. Here is his book. He by chance DID meet his hero. AND photographed him. AND stayed with him. AND watched and listened as Frank made *Hot Rats*, a Zappa classic. I won't go into *Hot Rats*, that's what this book is for. You will be amazed, kids.

– Billy Bob Thornton, Los Angeles, CA

THE
KID
IN
OHIO

The nutso, batshit crazy story of how

Bill Gubbins, a 19-year-old from Bowling Green,

Ohio, somehow ended up spending a

week with Frank Zappa in the summer of '69,

attended the key *Hot Rats* sessions, and

took the photos in this book.

Cheap thrills, chills, spills—and

a 1964 Dodge Polara.

Ahmet

In early January 2018, I was forwarded an email from Joe Travers, who we at Zappa Records lovingly call the "Vaultmeister," containing a PDF of a book prototype titled "August 1969 (An Intimate Look at the Recording of *Hot Rats*)" by a guy I'd never heard of named Bill Gubbins.

I looked through the prototype and very quickly thought to myself "holy shit balls these photos are amazing! Who the hell is this Bill Gubbins? And is it just me or does his last name sound like a fish? . . . Tonight's special is filet of gubbins, pan seared with a lemon caper sauce, served with a side of baby carrots." Anywho . . . This Bill dude had somehow been granted access into my father's musical wizarding world, and captured truly extraordinary photos of the mustachioed, mugician himself. I loved what I was seeing. Photos of Frank in all his creative glory looking to me like a total rock 'n' roll bad ass, moments of him hyper focused and other gems of Frank as happy as a clam, relaxed and casual. Bill didn't send a book prototype, what he really did was build a *Hot Rats* time machine with his camera lens. Fuck yeah! I knew then and there that I had to meet this Bill guy. So I sent the filet of Gubbins an email saying I'd very much like to chat with him in person if he was ever swimming around L.A. To my good fortune he replied. Within 24 hours a date had been set for us to meet up and a few weeks later, a joyful, silver-haired gentleman in his youthful 60s galloped into the Zappa homestead for what turned out to be one hell of a good time. I brewed up a strong pot of coffee and we sat around an imaginary fire pit and got to know one another. Bill wasn't part fish (to my disappointment) but he did come bearing gifts, which almost made up for the fact that he wasn't a merman. He brought large prints of his wonderful photographs and as we continued to exchange verbal niceties, what really turned out to be the most generous gift Bill could bring to a boy who misses his father every day of his life, was the amazing story of how he met Frank and the circumstances in which these photos came into existence. It was pretty clear after shooting the shit that fantastic afternoon, this story had to be shared.

So without further ado, here are the details of our first meeting and hopefully everyone's eyeballs will be teleported back to the year 1969.

Bill Gubbins . . . tell me how in the hell did you ever meet my dad?

YOU'RE PROBABLY WONDERING WHAT THE FISH IS GOING ON HERE

THE STORY OF THE STORY

An Interview by Ahmet Zappa with Bill Gubbins

Bill It's a wild story. I first met your father in Cleveland – Warrensville Heights, Ohio, to be exact – at a place called Musicarnival, on August 10, 1969, after what turned out to be the last U.S. show of the original Mothers of Invention.

A **And if memory serves, you said you gave my dad a ride back to where he was staying, right?**

B In my father's 1964 Dodge Polara I'd just been bequeathed for my 19th birthday.

A **That is so fucking awesome and so hard to imagine. You drove my father, a huge musician at the time –**

B He was.

A **And you gave him a ride, after the concert, back to his motel –**

B The Highlander Inn, and it's still there.

A **And you'd never met him before, he didn't know you, yet he trusted you to –**

B Get him to Motel 127 safely? Apparently. And I did.

A **And then he invited you to come to L.A. –**

B From Bowling Green, Ohio, just south of Toledo.

A **To attend some of the *Hot Rat*s sessions?**

B Yes. The last week of August 1969.

A **Wow, your story is bananas ...**

WHO'S "TUFFER"
AND
OTHER DILEMMAS
OF 1966.

To all the

Zappa fans

out there, our

"first-time" stories

are all the

same,

just the dates

and places

are different.

A   Shoot.

B   I'd like to start on the day I first encountered your father and his music. Because that's when the drive to meet him began.

A   Sounds reasonable. Let me fasten my seatbelt.

B   I think it's important for two reasons. First, it sets the scene and second, almost every Frank Zappa fan I've ever met has a very distinct memory of the powerful – even apocryphal – moment they first encountered your father and his music. He's never been "for everybody" – never will be, of course – but if you connected to him, you *really* connected to him.

I guess that's another way of saying, to all the Zappa fans out there, our "first-time" stories are all the same, just the dates and places are different.

A   Yeah. I think you're right. Keep going.

B   The year was 1966, the time was September, and the location was the Boardman Plaza, a strip mall in Boardman, Ohio, a suburb on the southern edge of a place called Youngstown, Ohio, which is equidistant from Cleveland and Pittsburgh. I had just turned 16 and was about to be a junior at Boardman High School.

I went there almost every Saturday afternoon with my best friend, Tom "Jake" Jacobs, and we were on a mission: A mission to find the latest records by the coolest groups. Especially the coolest *new* groups. And we had a special word to describe the coolest of the cool.

A   And that word was . . .

B   Tuff.

A   "Tuff"?

B   It's a great word, even your father used it.

A   I know.

B   This is one of the reasons I followed him so intently – and read every liner note, on every album – because he was always so *there*.

A   Explain.

B   So, to back up, we thought – or at least I thought – that somebody at Boardman High invented "tuff," but then, maybe on the back of *We're Only In It For the Money*, I saw the ad agency Frank had for awhile was named "Nifty" –

A   **"Tuff" –**

B   "& Bitchin'"!

A   **"Nifty, Tuff & Bitchin'" – But I think "tuff" is actually a California surfer term.**

B   Exactly. I guess we "culturally appropriated" it.

A   **[laughs] So, it's Saturday . . .**

B   And Tom and I are at Boardman Plaza . . . tuff-hunting.

We usually arrived around one or two and always started at the east end and then hit each of the stores that sold records, one by one.

A   **There was more than one record store? How many records stores were there?**

B   Only one – Record Rendezvous – but back then records were sold just about everywhere: Woolworths, W.T. Grants, Sears, even the local drug store, Gray Drugs, had a record rack.

A   **What's W.T. Grants?**

B   It was a relatively big national retailer then, but they bit the dust in the mid-'70s. I think the term back then was "variety" store – so think of it as a cross between the worst Wal-Mart and the best Dollar General you've ever been to.

A   **So, on this day, at that W.T. Grants . . .**

B   Tom and I enter and, near the center of the store, in the front, they have a single row of record bins with maybe five or six bins, each bin containing maybe 25 to 50 albums.

And, because there was no rhyme nor reason where they put the new albums, you had to flip through every album, every Saturday, in the hopes you found a new album or two.

A   **So you guys were basically insane . . . you were flipping through, maybe 200 or 250 individual albums, every week?**

B   At just one store.

So I'm flipping through the albums and – boom – I saw it!

A   *Freak Out!*?

B   No. The Fugs second album.

A   **Frank fucking loved the Fugs!**

B   They were a New York City group that was – in a kinda sorta way – the Mothers of the east coast. Kinda. Sorta.

A   **In your opinion. I don't know if I agree with that statement, but continue . . .**

B   So I'm having a really intense experience with this album cover because, among other things, it has a song titled "Squack-man Meets the Lunatic Vagina" and I'm having grand mal seizures because I've never seen the word "vagina" in print.

Which is when Jake turns to me and says, "Hey, look at *this*" and I turn to him and I see –

A   *Freak Out!*

B   Yes *FreakOut!*

A powerful moment for sure. I remember looking at the cover – staring at the cover – and wondering who this guy in the woman's fur coast was, what "freaking out" was, who Suzy Creamcheese from Salt Lake City was, what had "gotten into her," and, of course, what kind of music might possibly be on an album like this.

Fugs or Freak Out!

A **So you bought it?**

B Yes, but not before some careful consideration.

See, albums were pretty expensive back then – around $3 each – equivalent to $25 in 2019 – so Jake and I decided, if we found a really *tuff* album, we'd chip in $1.50 each and share it.

So there we were trying to make our big decision – Fugs or *Freak Out!* –

A **And I'm assuming you made the right decision here . . .**

B [laughs] Yes, we chose . . . *Freak Out!* Except, since he saw it first, Jake got to take it home first.

A **The bastard!**

B Then a couple of days later, it was my turn. And I was ready.

I had this weird record player with detachable speakers, so I put them on my bedroom floor, then stuck my damn head between them to listen to every cut on that album, as I read – and re-read – every word on the album cover and gatefold.

A **Seems like a giant set of earbuds.**

B Or, maybe "floorbuds."

A **Nice. But, wowie zowie, this chapter's running way over, so a summary statement if you would, Mr. G.**

B So all it took was *Freak Out!* and I was hooked. Plus, I was really, really curious to find out more about this Frank Zappa guy and what he would do . . . *next*.

A   Bill, put the time machine into fast forward and take us to 1969.

B   We've jumped from Boardman, Ohio, in the fall of 1966, to Bowling Green, Ohio, in the spring of 1969, where I was ending my freshman year at Bowling Green State University.

WELCOME TO . . . 1969
NEW YEAR'S RESOLUTION: INTERVIEW FRANK ZAPPA

A   Go on . . .

B   So Frank had sure fulfilled – and then some – his "what's next" promise, and the anticipation of each new album was now an important life marker.

And I spent much of the spring of 1969 centrally scrutinizing his latest, *Uncle Meat*. I was so into *Uncle*, in fact, that I listened to "Nine Types of Industrial Pollution" and tried to *count* the nine "types" I thought were hidden in the damn song! As if it was a piece of program music.

A   [laughs] Hilarious.

B   Around that time, I was starting to think career here, and I'd done some modest writing, radio shows, TV work, because I had a feeling that somewhere in the "media" was where I was meant to be.

In fact, as a big fan of *The Dick Cavett Show* then, I thought, you know, maybe I wouldn't be a bad interviewer.

A   Who doesn't dream of being a talk show host?! I get it. God knows, I dream of being a talk show host all day long.

B   Then I saw that the Mothers of Invention were playing in Cleveland, at a place called Musicarnival, in Warrensville Heights, on Sunday, August 10.

And I went: I'm going. And, by God, I'm going to interview Frank Zappa when I'm there!

A   I just love your teenage balls! Wait, that came out wrong. I just love, as a teenager, you're totally self-motivated to interview Frank. So awesome.

B   Uh, thank you? I asked around to see if any of my friends were interested in going but I really didn't get many takers – in fact, the only guy who was interested was a casual friend, and fellow Mothers/Zappa junkie named Dan Medsker, who worked with me

at the local PBS station (WBGU-TV). So in May or early June of 1969 I ordered four tickets.

A   How much were they?

B $5.00 each – which would be something like $40-$45 in 2019.

A   What a fucking bargain . . .

B   At any price.

I decided to stay in Bowling Green for the summer and got a job at the just-created BGSU Center for Popular Culture, one of the first, if not the first, departments at a major university devoted to the study of popular culture. Certainly a radical notion at the time because the average person – and certainly academics – didn't think anything in that realm was worthy of acknowledgement, let alone study.

The Center was started by a professor named Ray Browne and I worked for a pretty cool guy named Bill Schurk, who, as we'll soon see, plays a critical role in the narrative arc of our story.

A   Okay, so what about the interview?

B   Well, I asked the editor of the student newspaper, the *BG News,* how one would go about getting an interview with someone like Frank Zappa and he suggested – get ready – a "letter of introduction."

A   You snail-mailed that shit.

B   Yeah. So he typed up this crazy "To Whom It May Concern" letter of introduction – like something Lord Bullingdon might present in *Barry Lyndon* – and I was ready to go.

I had a Nikkormat 35mm camera with a standard 50mm lens, so the only thing left for my arsenal was a tape recorder, and, how I afforded it I have no idea, but I bought a crazy-big cassette player – one of the first boom-boxes, really – that had two mics and recorded in stereo. Damn thing weighed about 10 pounds, it was a nightmare to drag it around, but I got it.

A   Awesome

B   I was . . . ready.

9

WE'RE OFF TO SEE THE MOTHERS! AUGUST 10, 1969. THE DAY OF DESTINY IS HERE.

A **So this is your big day?**

B   Yup, it's Sunday, August 10, 1969.

So I pull the Polara out of Bowling Green and head east to Cleveland, where I pick up Dan and his friends and we're on our way to Warrensville Heights and Musicarnival where we're going to see the 7 PM show of the Mothers of Invention.

Now, as we're pulling in, I'm going to do a little more scene-setting, if I may.

A **Please do.**

B   Musicarnival was really a big tent — literally — so when you approached it was like arriving at the circus.

We get out of the Polara and I pack up all my gear: a 10-lb. boom box, the Nikkormat, a satchel with a notebook and all my other "serious interviewer" stuff.

A **I can see it now! I'll bet you were one cute kid!**

B   Uh, not exactly the self image I have from the period, but you're probably right.

Anyway, we approach the venue and see the aforementioned giant tent and, to its side, is a white building where the dressing rooms were and, on the other side, the venue concession stand.

As we get closer — and here's where it starts getting good — we see that, to the side of the building there's an open lawn area with picnic tables and stuff.

A **Why is this important?**

B   Because I have the eye-popping experience of seeing two of the Mothers — Don Preston and Motorhead Sherwood — hanging out there! In fact, Motorhead is on the ground filming Don with a Super8 camera.

A **Love it!**

B   Yes! And I even got close enough to take some not-bad photos of Motorhead filming Don.

Previous page

Don Preston (left) holding
a flower in the palm of his hand
as Jim "Motorhead" Sherwood
lets his Nikon roll.

Motorhead capturing the moment.

Frank ordering coffee.

Frank putting up with privacy invasion.

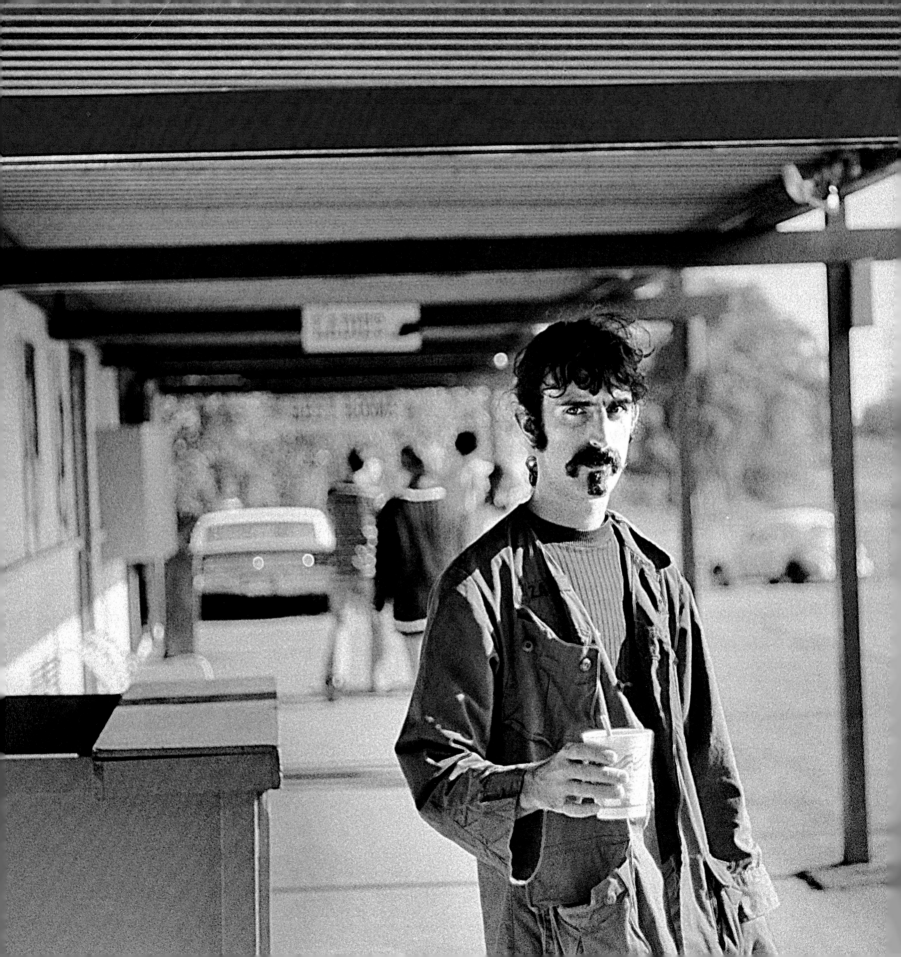

Ok, fine. Just let me have my coffee.

A   **You know, they're not too bad.**

B   From you, A., high praise indeed . . .

Then something dawned on me: If Don Preston and Motorhead Sherwood were hanging out with everyone, maybe . . . Frank Zappa might be around, too.

So I turned a corner to go to the concession stand and —

A   **Let me guess . . . And there he was.**

B   Yup. Standing alone, unnoticed, was the band leader of the headlining act of a sold-out concert in a major American city . . . buying his own cup of coffee.

A   **The man did love his coffee. Go on . . .**

B   Apparently not. [Begins waxing poetic] Why it was a different world back then, son, it was —

A   **Stick to the story. It's starting to get good. So there he was, right in front of everyone, what did you do?**

B   I became very nervous, I mean, was it supposed to be this easy?

I decided to get out the camera and start shooting, which I did, and got fairly close to him, but he really didn't pay much attention to me.

A   **So Frank was by himself? No one else was around?**

B   Nobody. And nobody even approached him, and in a couple of the photos, there are kids standing next to him, and you can tell, they don't have a clue.

But I have an easy theory of why they didn't.

A   **Go on . . .**

B   Because he was wearing his hair in a man bun!

A   **[laughs]**

B   Now I need to step back and contextualize this for you.

First, you have to understand how out there — I mean really, really, really *out there* — it was to have hair as long as Frank's and some of the other guys in the Mothers was. And I do mean dangerous "out there." Had somebody with hair that long simply walked down the street — any street — in Boardman or Youngstown back then they would have been harrassed almost instantly then shortly thereafter — very shortly thereafter — would have faced physical intimidation and probably an attack of some sort.

And it's not out of the realm of possibility that someone with hair that long might have been physically restrained while a couple of goombahs gave him a haircut. Long hair was that much an affront to their — in today's terminology — "toxic masculinity. "

A   **That is so fucked up.**

B   And my town was by no means the worst of the worst.

And then, if you upped the ante, and wore it in what today would be called a "man bun," which back then was something your *grandmother* wore under a *babushka* . . . I'm not sure what would have happened. But traffic would have been stopped.

A   **That's super lame people were like that back then.**

B   My point here is that the things we take for granted — you know, like men with man buns walking around unnoticed in, say, *Alabama* and the Florida *panhandle*, that acceptance was in no small part started by your father.

A   **My dad was the shit, bro. Miss him every day. So he's at the concession stand, getting his coffee, and then . . .**

B   As he's walking away, I take a pretty wide shot of him where he's looking at me as if I'm —

A   **About to fanboy gush vomit all over him?**

B   I guess, kind of. But then, after I take the shot, I go up to him and introduce myself.

The Mothers began a soundcheck while people were starting to come in — it was kind of crazy.

A So what did you say to him?

B I tell him I'm with the Bowling Green Center for Popular Culture and I'd like to interview him.

A And . . .

B He says he'll be doing press after the show and I should hunt down Dick Barber and tell him to let me in.

A This is what I love about Frank. It's so cool he gave you, this teenager, a shot.

B Yes, absolutely.

A For people who don't know, Dick Barber was his road manager then, so that makes sense.

B Yes. And, after my many hours — and hours — of album cover study and interview reading, not only did I know who Dick Barber was, I knew what he looked like. So off I went to find him.

A And . . .

B I did, introduced myself, made sure there was eye contact, and he nodded.

The next thing I remember was the Mothers began a soundcheck while people were starting to come in — it was kind of crazy.

I did get a couple of pics of the soundcheck, but then somebody saw me, asked me to stop, and I did.

A So tell me about the show . . .

"SILENCE FOOL, THIS IS CLEVELAND!" THE MOTHERS LIVE: AUDIENCE PARTICIPATION, "BACON FAT," A BIG DILEMMA, "TENT SHOW MUSIC #1," AND PROGRAM MUSIC EXPLAINED.

Previous page

Soundcheck.

Jimmy joins the check on drums.

A   **What was the show like?**

B   The show was fantastic, everything I'd dreamed it would be. And, if you don't believe me, you can hear it for yourself.

A   **Wait . . . You recorded it?**

B   Not only did I record it, I recorded it in *stereo*. It's pristine.

A   **You mean you just strolled in, with a huge boombox, nobody stopped you, and you recorded the show?**

B   And I was obvious about it. I put the box at my feet, held the two microphones one in each hand and handed them to Dan to hold while I was taking pictures.

A   **Do you still have the recordings?**

B   I think – *think* – I still have the original cassette tapes, but I'm not sure.

However, there is a complete copy of the show and all my interviews at the Bowling Green Center for Popular Culture. They sent me files of everything so I could us them for the book.

I've checked around, BTW, and I think mine is the only recording of the show – I've never encountered another. It must be because all the set lists you see online are wrong, way wrong.

A   **How so?**

B   Well, for starters, none of the set lists include Frank singing Andre Williams' "Bacon Fat" and Jimmy Carl Black singing "Big Leg Emma," both of which were fantastic.

Frank also did some unbelievable audience participation pieces where he taught the audience his basic hand signals – middle finger up for a high "peep," middle finger down for a low "poot," then the vomiting noises, etc.

Then – certainly the coolest part – since the audience surrounded the band, he walked around and conducted them in 360-degree surround stereo. They also did an improv piece that, when it was done, Frank told the audience it was called, "Tent Show Music #1."

He also did a great intro to "A Pound For a Brown on the Bus," that referenced "program music." All in all – simply fantastic. And it holds up very well, which is doubly awesome because of the historic nature of the show.

B   It was the last U.S. show of the original line-up of the Mothers of Invention. They did one more show in Canada later that week, but then that was it – he broke up the group in early September, just after I left my California visit.

Which is why, among all the photos I took, I might be proudest of this photo that has everybody wailing out, "The Last U.S. Show of the Original Mothers."

A   **That picture is epic.**

B   There's something else about this photo I'd like to point out, especially contrasting our times with those of fifty years ago.

Look at that photo and tell me what you see.

A   **Is this a trick question?**

B   No.

A   **I see one of the greatest bands of all time on a circular stage surrounded by what appears to be a sold-out audience. How'd I do?**

B   Good. Now look at the photo again –

A   **Ok . . . what am I missing?**

B   Do you see any security people, especially around the stage?

The show begins.
From left to right, they are:
Don Preston, keyboards;
Jimmy Carl Black, percussion;
Art Tripp III, percussion;
Roy Estrada, bass;
Motorhead Sherwood, tambourine;
Bunk Gardner, saxophone;
Buzz Gardner, trumpet;
Ian Underwood, saxophone;
and Frank Zappa, guitar.

nstrumental.

A   No, that is crazy.

B   Exactly. And notice how low the stage is? Maybe – what? – three or four feet off the ground?

A   If that.

B   Not sure this is a grand point, but it's an interesting one: In 1969, a major rock act could play in front of 2,500 people, on a very low stage, with no real escape route if things got ugly – in other words, they'd be surrounded – without a single – a single – security person in sight.

And during a show that lasted over two hours, not one person tried to get on that stage. Not one.

Now I'm not saying it was a good thing there weren't any security people in front of the stage, I'm just saying things were more civilized then, even for the audience of a pretty provocative group. The social contract was simply stronger.

Imagine that today?

A   I can't. That's fucking nuts.

B   Alright, enough of that, the show's over and I've got a press conference to get to.

A   Yeah, come on Bill, seriously . . . What the hell are you waiting for?

Frank leading everyone into an instant
composition he dubbed "Tent Show Music #1."

Following page
The aural Mothers energy.

THE POST-SHOW PRESS CONFERENCE TOUCHES ON STRAVINSKY, SELF-DEFENSE, BABIES WITH WINGS, AND THE MOON LANDING.

B   Okay, Ahmet, are you ready? Cause things are going to *really* start kickin' in now.

A   **Hold on . . . let me do a huge line of imaginary blow to prepare myself – *snnnerriff!* – ok I'm locked in and jacked to the gills on unicorn dust. Let's do this.**

B   So the Mothers show ended, I grabbed my big boom box, my Nikkormat, my satchel, and started fighting my way out of there to get to the press conference. This was it! My destiny! To interview Frank Zappa! It was like I'd been shot out of a cannon.

It wasn't easy, and I didn't want to knock anyone over, but – and forgive the mild melodrama – I'd been waiting for this moment for a long time, and –

A   **You weren't about to be dee-nied!**

B   That's right!

I got out to the circular concourse and tried to figure out where the damn backstage was, which wasn't easy.

Then I found it, there was Dick, he pulled the canvas aside like it was a curtain – kinda like that famous Charles Willson Peale painting, *The Artist in His Museum*—and boom, there I was.

A   **So rad! What was the *scene* like?**

B   It was a pretty funky backstage area, there were the typical dressing-room tables with makeup lights, a couple of rows of lockers, and Frank was sitting in a folding wooden chair talking to between five and ten people, while the other Mothers were hanging out behind the row of lockers.

I was a little perturbed, cause the press conference . . . had started . . . without me!

A   **The damn nerve of these savages.**

B   I assessed the situation pretty quickly and sat as close to Frank as I could, just to his left, and set up the recorder.

There was only one "real journalist" that I knew, and that was the *Cleveland Plain Dealer*'s legendary Jane "The world's oldest teenager" Scott; everyone else seemed to have a random feel to them –

Backstage post-show press conference.

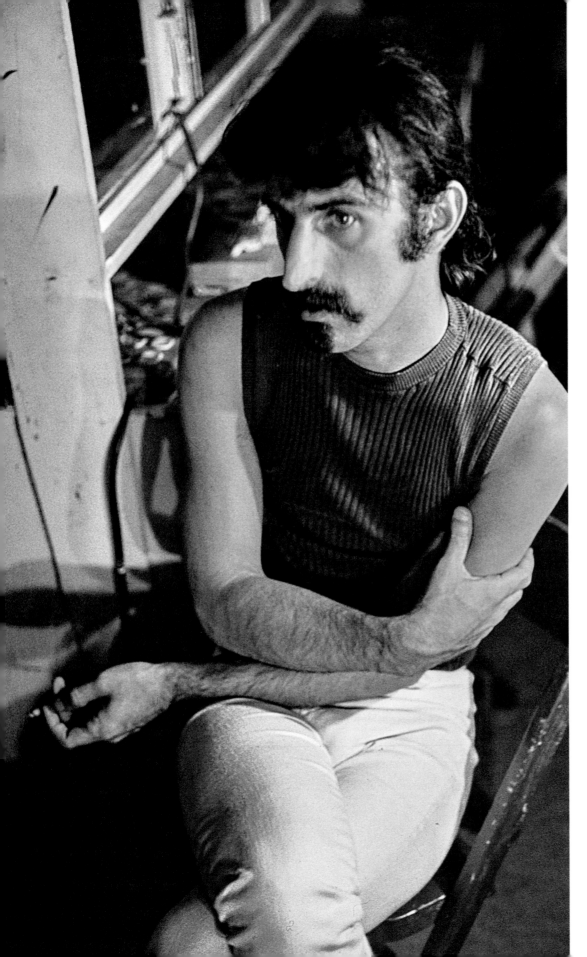

Seriously?

I thought it was badly directed as a TV special.

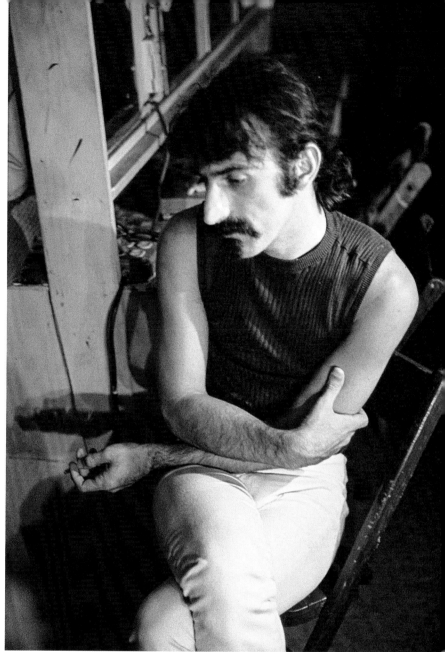

Time to go.

The Shave.

Sit? Stand? Watch?

A **Even you I bet.**

B Sad to say, yes.

My hindsight memory of the event was that the other questions weren't that good, but as I listened to the tape after nearly 50 years, I had to come to the sad conclusion that maybe – just maybe – I wasn't necessarily the smartest person in the room.

A **Aww . . . I think you can give yourself a break.**

B Well maybe, but the questions did have a dated, pro-forma feel to them: somebody asked him about drugs, another about revolution, and another about religion – which, to me, wasn't as interesting as asking him about his music.

But he had the kind of mind that could fashion an interesting answer no matter what you asked him. In fact, his best line of the night was his answer to the question, "Frank, what did you think of the moon landing?"

A **This should be good.**

B It was. He said, deadpan, perfect timing, "I thought it was badly directed as a TV special."

A **Hilarious.**

B And brilliantly insightful. As things progressed, I started feeling comfortable – in other words, even if not the *smartest* person in the room, I wasn't the *dumbest*. So I summoned all my courage and finally asked him a question.

I asked him how he wrote music, what was his process.

He warmed to it, gave a good answer that was also funny, we seemed to connect; so alright, I'm off to the races. I started asking him questions about Stravinsky, how he handled being hassled, if he read music magazines, and he gave great answers to each.

But listen carefully, please, here's the good part.

A **I'm listening.**

B At about this time, from behind the lockers, one of the Mothers – probably Ian Underwood – stuck his head in and said something like, "Hey Frank, we're going back to the motel, you can either come with us, or maybe one of these people can give you a – "

I had no idea this was coming, but in a damn nanosecond I knew: this was my shot and I went for it.

So without skipping a beat, and taking complete control of the situation, I said, "Frank, I'll give you a ride back."

A **That was ballsy!**

B So Frank looks at me, looks back at Ian, then says, "Go ahead, I'll ride back with him."

A **How unbelievable and weird all at the same time! I'm astonished that he trusted you.**

B Agreed.

A **No for real . . . that is seriously bonkers to me. Then what happened?**

B So the press conference keeps going for a few minutes, but is clearly running out of steam, so at a brief lull I really grabbed the bull by the horns, looked at Frank, and said, "You ready to go?"

He looked at me and said, "Sure. Let's go. I'll get my briefcase and meet you outside."

And that was the end of the press conference.

A **I cannot get enough of this story, it's the *Twilight Zone* also . . . total sidebar, I love that Frank always carried a briefcase . . . So not rock.**

B Exactly. So I grab my boombox, my camera, my satchel and headed out to parts unknown.

Not Watch?

A   So you're in your Polara

B   Not so fast, we gotta get there first.

So I pack up, and as I head for the backstage exit, a terrifying thought hits me.

A   What?

B   In the excitement of the press conference, I realized I'd completely – and I do mean completely – abandoned my three friends for the hour I was backstage. They were stuck outside, unsure exactly where I was or what I was doing, completely stranded, with no direction home.

You a *Curb Your Enthusiasm* fan, Ahmet?

A   Of course I am.

B   Well, when I opened that canvas curtain, there they were, staring at me with spit in their eyes, just like Jeff's wife Susie waiting in the driveway when Jeff and Larry think they've pulled something over on her.

A   Yikes!

B   Now Dan was a pretty mellow guy but my memory is that mellow was something he was not at that moment.

A   So they were pissed and thought you were being Mr. Big Shot, hanging out with their hero while you left them behind?

B   Couldn't have said it better myself.

I'm trying to explain the situation to Dan, who's having none of it, when I notice he starts glancing behind my right shoulder, then gets a look on his face as if Godzilla's approaching with an M-15.

A   It's Frank, right?

B   Oh yeah. I turn back, Frank's approaching, smiling, with his briefcase, then I turn back to Dan, whose face now reads less of fear and more of someone who's been tazed –

A   Ha! He got wowie zowied.

B   So I now introduce him to my three mind-blown colleagues and your father is his usual extremely polite self, and we all head off to the Polara, which is now the only car in a completely empty parking lot.

As we start walking, my heart's beating and my mind's racing with just a few of the following thoughts: 1. I have no idea how to get to the Highlander Inn. 2. How do I keep the conversation going without things getting silent-weird? 3. What if I get into some terrible accident and everyone is killed but me and I have to live with the life-long stigma of being the piss-poor driver who killed Frank Zappa?

But that fear's kind of negated by the next one: 4. Given the stress, I'm not sure I remember how to *drive*.

A   Fuckin-A!

B   [laughs]

And, speaking of racing thoughts, as we approach the car, I'm now in my next existential dilemma: Should I unlock *his* door first – as if I were on a date – or would it be rude if I unlock the driver's-side door *first* and *then* open the lock from the *inside*.

A   What did you do?

B   I can't remember.

A   [laughs]

B   Now we're in the car, we pull out, I'm blanking on how we got there, but I think Frank knew the directions. (Which given his extremely high level of all-around competency, doesn't surprise me.)

Now, desperate to keep the conversation going, I'm asking him everything I can think of, and, just as I'm starting to run out of ideas, Dan and his pals realize that since Frank is so damn friendly, they might as well start asking questions, too, which they do.

And Frank likes their questions, gives them good answers, and suddenly the car is filled with five great friends, happily yakking it up, comparing notes on the music of their favorite group, except one of the guys is the one who created it!! And it seems as if he's having as good a time talking about it as we are.

A   Love it!

B   So we pull into the Highlander Inn about 11:30 and, given it's a Sunday night, the parking lot is *empty*. Frank tells me where his room is and I pull into a parking space near it.

"WE'RE GIVING FRANK A RIDE TO THE MOTEL." "OK, SUR – WHAT?!?" A ROCK SUPERSTAR AND FOUR FANS, IN A '64 DODGE POLARA, JUST CRUISIN' FOR THE HIGHLANDER INN LATE ON A SUNDAY NIGHT. WISH YOU WERE THERE. (ROD SERLING SURE WAS.)

We're all still yakking and I'm thinking: If it goes no further than this, I can still die a happy man. But then Frank does something very interesting, he swivels his body and turns towards us with his back against the door. To which I respond by turning the ignition off.

A   **You're in for the long haul – excellent!**

B   Exactly. So we're all talking and maybe 15 minutes later somebody says, "Frank, what's your next album?" To which he says, "It's called *Hot Rats*, want to come up and see the cover?"

A   **Shut up . . . So you go right?**

B   Well, of course we do. The four of us get out of the Polara and follow him to his room on the first floor of the otherwise totally deserted Highlander Inn.

A   **No groupies, no band members, nobody?**

B   The place is more deserted than the stage set for *Waiting for Godot*.

He opens the door, we enter and then he pulls out a printer's proof of the *Hot Rats* cover, which is amazing – and extremely professional – to me because I'd never seen a printer's proof before.

But I realized that this thing had run its course – I mean, what were we going to do, "Hey, Frank, wanna see what's on TV?" – and since I couldn't bear the thought of him ending it, I said, "Frank, we can't thank you enough, but I need to get these guys home, and I need to drive back to Bowling Green."

However, I did throw this in as we were starting to leave: "Just know I'd love to interview you for the Center for Popular Culture, so if – "

And then he says: "What are you doing tomorrow?"

I don't know if I even answered, but he continues and says, "We have a day off and we're just hanging around here, so why don't you come back and we'll do the interview then."

A   **Unbelievable.**

B   Yeah. So I asked him what time, he said noon, and I said, "I'll be here."

So, we left – and I'm sure we whooped and hollered when we finally got in the car – I dropped the guys off, made the three-hour drive back to Bowling Green, got maybe two hours of sleep, then got up, drove into work about eight, asked Bill Schurk if I could have the day off to interview Frank Zappa, he said sure as long as we can get a copy of the tape. No problem, of course. So I hit the road back to the Highlander Inn..

A   This is an epic story.
B   We got a long way to go until it peaks, a long way to go.

LET'S GO SWIMMING! WITH THE MOTHERS OF INVENTION! AT THE HIGHLANDER INN. (AND THEN DO THE WORST FRANK ZAPPA INTERVIEW – EVER!)

Swimming with the Mothers.

B   So I pull into the Highlander Inn almost exactly at noon, and am standing at the green door to Frank's room wondering, am I really going to knock?

A   You did, of course, yes?

B   It was strange, but I did. And from inside I hear, "Who is it?" To which I answer, "Uh, it's Bill Gubbins, you remember, the guy from last night you invited to come back and do the interview with."

Frank opens the door, smiles, and says, "C'mon in, I'm shaving."

A   So weird.

B   So he's in the bathroom shaving, with the door open, and I'm really at DEFCON 10 of awkwardness: Do I sit on the bed? In a chair? Stand there? Watch him? Not watch him? Make conversation? Be silent?

The only thing I could think to do — which was actually pretty stupid — was take pictures of him shaving in the mirror outside the bathroom door.

A   Did you ask him if you could?

B   I don't remember, but I'm pretty sure I did.

He finishes, we walked to the pool, and there, cavorting and splashing as if they were five years old, were Jimmy Carl Black, Ian Underwood, Don Preston, and Motorhead Sherwood.

A   What a shock for the tourists!

B   And then some. Except for Don, they all had hair down to the middle of their backs, several in ponytails, which, to the typical tourists from, say, Findlay, Ohio, on their way to, say, Niagara Falls, was a sight to behold, I'm sure.

But everybody was cool, and there weren't any hassles.

Of course, I can't say I paid much attention, given that I was about to start my big interview.

A   And . . .

B   There are certain times you're up to the challenge and certain times you're not. My track record was pretty good over the last 12 hours, but I done ran outta gas.

A   What do you mean?

B   Well, think about it: I had Frank Zappa's complete and undivided attention — for at least two hours or more if it went well — in a totally relaxed atmosphere with no distractions, not a single one. No phone calls, no planes to catch, no obligations, no sessions to get to, nothing. It's Warrensville Heights, Ohio at noon on a sleepy August Monday! What's he going to do? Go to the Terminal Tower? See if Sam McDowell is pitching that day at Municipal Stadium?

I don't know, but I'm guessing there weren't many interviewers in Frank's *life* who had that ideal a set-up.

A   Oh shit, I'm sensing trouble.

B   Not so much trouble as stupidity.

So here I have him, he's all mine, he's ready, here I go, so guess — just try — what my first question was?

A   You are killing me. I have no idea. What the fuck did you ask?

B   My first question was, and I quote, "Was the cover of *We're Only In It For The Money* a parody of *Sgt. Pepper*?"

It's Warrensville Heights at noon.

A   Ooof. What was his answer?

B   He looked me right in the eye and said, as droll as can be, "I'm glad you got that."

A   Ouch. So then what happened?

B   I carried on, best as I could, and the interview went on for another hour or so. The rest wasn't bad, but wasn't good. I finished up and he actually walked me back to his room or the car, I can't remember which, and, as we were walking, I said I'd still like to continue the interview, and then the shock came.

A   What?

B   He asked if I wanted to come out to Los Angeles in a couple of weeks to finish the interview and attend the final *Hot Rats* sessions.

A   Well dude, the interview couldn't have been that bad if he asked you to visit him in Los Angeles.

B   I guess so.

A   You do realize how apeshit crazy your story is right?

B   Stay tuned, Ahmet, stay tuned.

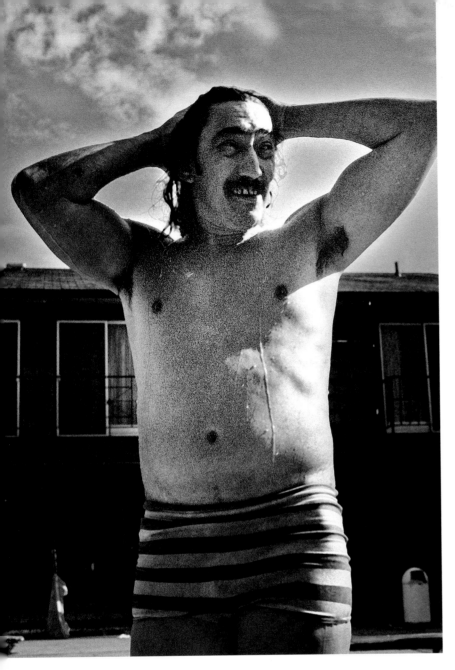

Jimmy Carl Black—Pool Stripes.

Ian Underwood—Wet.

42

Motorhead—Buff.

Highlander Inn Livin'.

Smoking and smiling poolside at the Highlander Inn.

Squint puff.

$210 for the round-trip direct flight from Toledo, to Los Angel

"HEY, MOM AND DAD, MIND IF I SPEND A WEEK IN L.A. WITH FRANK ZAPPA? YEAH, R-R-RIGHT, IT'S THE POSTER YOU HATE, THE PHI ZAPPA KRAPPA GUY, B-B-B-BUT, UH, COULD YOU PAY FOR THE FLIGHT OUT THERE ANYWAY?" . . .

Ohio
es.

A   Alright ... keep going.

B   So I'm back at Bowling Green and I have to figure out how to get the $210 for the round-trip direct flight from Toledo, Ohio to Los Angeles.

A   And your choices are . . .

B   My parents.

A   [laughs] So, how hard was that?

B   Well, $210 was a lot of money back then, maybe $1,500 in 2019, and we were middle class — my father was a loan officer at a small bank and my mother worked as a secretary at Boardman High — so it wasn't crazy, but an "ask" nonetheless.

A   How'd it go?

B   Though they were staunch Republicans, they were what was then known as "Rockefeller Republicans," which meant they were fiscally conservative but generally socially liberal. Such a distinction really doesn't exist today.

So they knew who Frank was, primarily from the Phi Zappa Krappa poster I had in my room, and they thought it was crude, but it's not like they forbid it or ripped it down in the middle of the night.

Even though they thought the invitation was strange, and didn't quite understand it, they at least knew it was a pretty big opportunity.

A   They fronted you the money?

B   Yes. A gesture for which I'll be forever grateful.

They only last thing I had to do was confirm with Frank that, yes, I was coming, it was cool, and the dates were good.

Frank had given me his assistant Pauline Butcher's card, so I called her, she put me right through to Frank . . . He remembered me, we locked in the dates.

A   Impressive. So then off to L.A.?

B   Off to L.A.

47

A   So it's the big day, you wake up and then what?

B   Yes, the big day: I'm going to . . . Frank Zappa's house!

A   [laughs] Start talkin'.

B   I got up around 4 AM in the Ohio-gothic boarding house I lived in on the south side of Bowling Green, finished packing my enormous cheap plastic beige Samsonite suitcase, and then Dave Kresak, my roommate, drove me to the Toledo airport for the direct flight from Toledo to L.A.

A   Were you nervous?

B   Hell yes I was. Even though I'd spoken to Frank, he'd given me the address, it was all good, I was still worried that this wasn't some giant hallucination and I'd have the front door slammed in my face when I got there.

A   I understand. Was this your first time to Los Angeles?

B   No, I went once before in the summer of 1966 for a family vacation but this trip was an entirely different animal. The plane landed around 9:30 PST, got through baggage claim and grabbed a cab for . . .

A   7885 Woodrow Wilson Drive!

B   Yes. The same house you grew up in.

A   So, as you're sitting in the cab heading to the house, what did you think of L.A. this time as an older teenager on a mission?

B   Strange, surreal — but I was still too worried about whether anyone would let me in to really appreciate the wonders of La Cienega Boulevard.

Plus, it was brutally hot — at least to someone coming from northwestern Ohio — and I was way overdressed; I think I even had a T-shirt on under my shirt. And the cab didn't have air-conditioning.

A   That must have sucked.

B   So finally, after about 45 minutes, there we were, pulling into your driveway. The first thing I thought was how *normal* your house looked.

A   What were you expecting . . . ?

B   I'm not really sure — I certainly didn't think he'd live in a, I dunno, a geodesic *dome* or some crazy *teepee*, but on the other hand, I didn't think he'd live in a house similar to one a friend of mine like Larry Hageman might live in on Meadowbrook Avenue back in Boardman.

The only clue that it wasn't completely normal were the two huge doors carved into the basement wall.

A   I know those doors well. They were always bringing amplifiers and equipment in and out of there through them. So you're in the driveway, in the cab —

B   And I'm nervous as shit. So nervous, in fact, I asked the cabbie if he'd wait until I knew I could get in. He said he couldn't. Sweating profusely, I exit the cab with the huge cheap plastic beige Samsonite suitcase, looking like the nerd I was, trying to summon the courage to walk up and ring Frank Zappa's doorbell.

As I watched the cab back out of your driveway and head out, I realized my last means of escape had just disappeared into the morning heat.

A   OK, so?

B   Even though your house was — at most — maybe 30 yards away, by the time I dragged that damn Samsonite up your front walk I looked like I'd walked through a monsoon to get there.

A   [laughs]

B   I got to your front door, stared at the doorbell, then rang it not once, but — and don't ask me why — *twice*. Ding-dong. Ding-*dong*. And then I waited.

A   How long until somebody came?

B   It seemed like an eternity, then, finally, I heard footsteps approach, the sound of the doorknob turning, and the door opened to reveal . . . None other than . . . Janet Ferguson.

A   I hear she was cool, I don't think I ever met her. So Janet opens the door . . .

7885 WOODROW WILSON DRIVE.
IS ANYBODY HOME IN THERE?

"He's a-*sleep*!"

B   And I can only imagine her POV — a dorky kid, sweating profusely, with that god-awful, huge beige ugly plastic Samsonite next to him.

A   What did she say?

B   I think she said "What do *you* want?" But she might have also said, "What the *fuck* do *you* want?"

A   [laughs] I'm gonna go with the latter. So what did you say?

B   Probably something like, "Uh-uh-uh-HI! I'm B-B-B-Bill Gubbins from B-B-B-Bowling Green, Ohio, and Frank Z-Z-Z-Zappa invited me to come and s-s-s-stay with h-h-h- him."

A   [laughs]

B   To which she replied, almost shouting, "He's a-*sleep*!"

I have to be honest, Ahmet, even though I knew he was a rock star; an adult, asleep, at 10 in the morning, it really threw me. I mean, in my neighborhood as a kid, if somebody's father was asleep at 10 in the morning, they probably would have, I dunno, called the Boardman Police or something.

A   Dude, my dad lived by a very different set of rules.

B   [laughs] Of this I know. So Janet and I stared at each other, neither one of us knowing quite what to do or say, then she said, "I'll check with Gail," and closed-slammed the door.

A   She left you outside???

B   Yes she did and there I stood. For a long, long time. The perspiration slowly winding its way down my forehead. My Samsonite at my side.

A   Dude you're grossing me out with your sweat and if you say Samsonite again, I might have to kill you.

B   [laughs] So then I heard the footsteps again, the door opened, and Janet — none too happy about it — said, "It's okay with Gail. Come on in."

A   **You did it, you made it in in.**

B   Yes indeed. The first room. The first room I entered following Janet was the purple living room that would later be featured in the famous 1971 *Life* magazine photo essay, "Rock Stars and Their Parents."

Then we went through some French doors into your dining room, where I had one of the biggest shocks of the whole damn trip.

A   **I can't wait to hear . . .**

B   You ready? Folded laundry – on the dining room table. Neatly – and I mean neatly – folded laundry on the dining room table. Just like my Aunt Larabelle did back in Boardman. It blew my mind. Gail Zappa, hippest of the hip, put her folded laundry on the dining room table just like Laurabelle, who I don't think would take offense – in fact, she might consider it a compliment – at being called "squarest of the square."

In the end, maybe that's our great human unifier –

A   **Oh yeah. Growing up, Gail doing laundry was actually a thing. Nobody but her was allowed to do it and if you fucked with those rules, well then may god have mercy on your soul.**

B   [laughs] Then we walked into the kitchen where there was your mom, Janet, and Miss Lucy from the GTOs.

A   **So cool.**

B   Indeed. Though none of them were that much older than I was, it's almost impossible to comprehend how far out of my league I was.

A   **Yeah, well all three of those women were total bad asses! So what did you do next?**

B   I hid. In plain sight. There was a wooden breakfast nook in the kitchen and I remember sliding in and staring at my thumb, while I nursed endless Pepsi's and chain-smoked Winstons. There was much exchanging of gossip among the three, none of it salacious, though Jeff Beck's name was mentioned a couple of times.

Oh, and I can't forget that your sister, the almost-two Moon Unit was wandering around in the midst of it all, quite cheerfully, as I remember. I also went outside and walked up the short hill to the small pool that was being cared for by Frank's brother Carl. Then went back.

I sat in the kitchen for maybe two hours until I got "rescued" by Kansas, the Mothers roadie.

A   **Kanzus J. Kanzus?**

B   One and the same, certainly a man of many names.

Kansas had either been alerted to my estrogenal plight or wandered into the kitchen for something and, having pity on this lost soul, volunteered to take me down to the basement.

A   **A ton of magic happened down there.**

B   That damn nails it for sure.

So I followed Kansas back out of the kitchen, passing the wonderful folded laundry – which, BTW, contained the original of Frank's legendary T-shirts, either "Pipco" or "Rental," I'm not sure which – back through the purple living room, and across from the front door, down the stairs that lead down into . . . the basement.

A   **That basement was really an early version of The Utility Muffin Research Kitchen. The house changed so much over the years.**

B   Well the room I was in was long and rectangular, and went under much of the length of the house. At the far end was Frank's work area, with a long table where he composed, wrote, edited film, and even looked at photos on a built-in light box.

Off to the left was a two-track Scully (on which, a few days later, I watched him edit "Peaches en Regalia" down from the longer original version) with a small closet next to it that held Frank's record collection, most of which was sitting on the floor.

The rest of the basement had a big sofa on the left –

A   **I remember the late-1970s version of that space very well. I totally get what you are describing.**

B   And in front of the sofa was a small coffee table stacked with an incredible collection of Frank's personal memorabilia – including,

I do believe, the original of his high school graduation photo that was used on the back cover of *Ruben & the Jets*.

Then, on the right wall, in the midst of a row of amplifiers, were the big double doors.

In a way — and I know this might sound corny — but to be down there was, in a way, to be in the center of your father's brain.

A [laughs] Probably true, makes a lot of sense. So what next?

B Well, I did what any self-respecting Zappa fan would do — I rummaged through it all!! But, of course, very carefully, very gently, and very respectfully, especially considering I was down there alone for long stretches of time, maybe even an hour or more on a couple of occasions.

A Really? That seems so nuts to me. You could have just walked out with all of it, right?

B Well, the Samso — sorry, my luggage was certainly big enough.

Maybe it was me, maybe it was the times, maybe both, but I have to tell you that thought never even occurred to me. And I don't think it would have occurred to most people back then. Make of that what you will.

A Well I'm glad you didn't steal stuff, but back to the story.

B I hung out there with Kansas, who was in and out, for a couple of hours, and then, around 5 PM, down the stairs, ready to start a brand-new day, walked you know who.

Frank greeted me warmly, and, I think the first thing he said was, "Want to come to a teenage recording session tonight?"

But I politely said, "Frank, thanks for the offer, but I'd rather sit down here and study old photos of the Blackouts and peruse yellowing newspaper clippings of your playing-the-bike bit on *The Steve Allen Show*, if you don't mind."

A I call bullshit.

B You're right. Who in their right mind could turn down a "teenage recording session" with Mr. Z.?

There was some hanging out, then, around 5:30 or 6, carefully portioned plates of food magically appeared from Gail's kitchen above, we ate in the basement, and then it was time to head to the studio for the 7 PM session.

A

Now the real adventure begins.

THE TH
THE
KID HO
IN RA
L.A. SE

E

T

TS

SSIONS

A Let's make sure nobody's lost here. So are you losing your mind that you're going to the studio with Frank?

B Hell, damn yes. Acclimatization has taken place, and I'm sitting in the back seat of the Zappa family Buick on our way to attending my first *Hot Rats* session at Whitney Studio in Glendale, California.

The car is being driven, I believe, by Frank's brother Carl, and Frank, who didn't drive, is sitting in the passenger seat as we wind our way up and down Mulholland Drive toward Glendale.

A Carl and Frank. The dynamic duo.

B I will always defer to you on familial matters; I was too busy with the dynamics of getting my eyeballs back into their sockets. To one accustomed to the flat, flat flatlands of northwestern Ohio, this drive over, under, sideways, down the curves of Mulholland confirmed: I definitely wasn't in Defiance, Ohio anymore.

So, we pull into Whitney Studio, which was in a fairly nondescript building in the midst of Glendale's other nondescript buildings on West Glenoaks Boulevard. Carl drops us off and I follow Frank into the studio; it's around 6:45.

We pass the studio's 9-5ers, secretaries, assistants, tape-duplicators, all finishing up the day's work before heading home.

We land in the control room, with a pretty large console shoehorned into a room filled with tape machines of all configurations, floor-to-ceiling racks of power equipment and such, and the worn and rickety Naugahyde chairs near the console. (Keep on eye on these chairs, they will be a plot point soon.)

Already there was Ian Underwood, the multi-instrumental overdub virtuoso who played, at least 13 *different* instruments on *Hot Rats* (14 if you count his finger snaps on "It Must Be a Camel").

To watch him record — as we soon will — all the horn parts to "Peaches en Regalia," one after another, effortlessly, nailing each in maybe two of three takes at most, was very impressive — at least to someone whose experience watching horn players was limited to the Mothers show in August and numerous performances of the Boardman High School Marching Band conducted by Dick Bame.

Also there was engineer Dick Kunc.

I gotta say, you captured a side of my father that most photographers never even came close to.

A By then a veteran of multiple Mothers albums, who, if memory serves, at that time, held the title of "Head of Engineering" for Bizarre and Straight Records, Frank's two labels.

B Dick was obviously under some degree of pressure, especially given the challenges of Frank's attention to the minutest of sonic details as well as engineering one of the first albums recorded in 16-track, so I didn't engage with him the same way I did with Frank and Ian.

A I so wish I could have been a fly on the wall.

B And, once the staff left, it was just the four of us, which was the way it was for all the sessions, save for the "babysitter" from the Mormon Church, a nice guy who joined us for part of the last Whitney session a couple of days later.

A Time out. What does the Mormon Church have to do with the *Hot Rats* sessions?

B Whitney Studio was founded and owned by the Mormon Church — at least until it was purchased by MCA in the '70s (it's now MCA Whitney, and still operates at the same address). In fact, a not-insignificant reason why Frank chose Whitney as one of the three studios where *Hot Rats* was recorded (Sunset Sound and T.T.G. were the others) was because of the large Whitney pipe organ. Dubbed "Organus Maximus" by the studio's Mormon founder, Lorin J. Whitney, its grandeur can be most clearly heard on "Son of Mr. Green Genes" and, to a lesser extent, on "Peaches en Regalia."

There are several photos of Ian playing the organ when they wheeled it in close to control room, and it can be seen, usually in the far left back, in any wide shot of the studio from the control room.

It's worth noting Frank had been using Whitney for at least a year before *Hot Rats* and – get ready for this one – all the studio sessions for Captain Beefheart's *Trout Mask Replica* were done there.

A **Bill, I gotta say I knew you were a Zappa fan but your attention to detail and knowledge of Frank runs deep. I'm loving this. So tell me more about what was it like for you, a total outsider, to be at the sessions? I mean, did you know anything about recording studios, did Frank set any ground rules – what about taking pictures, any boundaries on those?**

B   I'd never been in a recording studio before Whitney so I was very careful not to do – or touch – anything that might be remotely problematic, and I never did. I moved slow and smooth (you will hear the tragic exception shortly, stay tuned).

As for the photos, I asked Frank if it was cool if I shot, he said it was, and I was careful not to intrude. If you look at the photos carefully, you'll see very few are full-on frontal, they're just off to one side or the other. Neither Frank nor Ian minded, but I didn't get too many of Dick, simply because he was so busy and concentrating so intensely.

Everyone was pretty comfortable with me shooting, especially Frank, and I got pretty close to him a couple of times. Maybe it was me not seeming like a "real" photographer (which I wasn't and have never been), maybe because the Nikkormat with the standard issue 50mm lens didn't look the kind of camera a "real photographer" like Ed Caraeff or Jim Marshall would have, or maybe it was because I was so unobtrusive and amateurish that they figured I probably didn't even have film in the camera, who knows?

ATTACK OF THE WHITNEY **SESSION** 1 STUDIO CHICKEN SOUP. CAN THERE BE ANYTHING MORE EMBARRASSING, ON YOUR FIRST NIGHT AT A BIG-TIME RECORDING SESSION? IT TASTED GOOD, THOUGH.

A **Bro, I gotta say, you captured a side of my father that most photographers never even came close to. It's amazing to me. You were basically creeping around the studio like a tarantula with your keen eyes and you were getting these amazing shots. There had to have been something about your personality that really gelled with Frank. What an incredibly intimate situation. You would not have been allowed there unless Frank felt the trust. I'm blown away by all this. Really how in the hell did you do it?**

B   I have no idea, because I'd never done anything like it before. Maybe it was beginner's luck. I never asked anyone to pose, so everyone – especially Frank – was very human, very real. Nobody put on any airs, that's for sure. Maybe the sessions were so relaxed that nobody cared. I just somehow got the shots.

Frank at the Whitney board.

Cuing up the 16-track.

Behind the glass.

To pipe or not to pipe.

He was playing this great solo, and I was standing mere inches from him . . .

That brings me to something else about the sessions worth mentioning and that's how efficient and low-key they were. There was an enormous amount recorded while I was there – the majority of "Peaches en Regalia," "Son of Mr. Green Genes," "Little Umbrellas," and "It Must Be a Camel" – yet there wasn't a single moment of anxiety or tension I saw.

A   How did Frank run the sessions?

B   Effortlessly. Everyone seemed to know what to do, and when to do it, but I don't recall anyone being *told* or *directed* in any explicit manner. Things just seemed to *happen*. Granted, the three of them had worked together for a couple of years.

A   So where did you sit?

B   I started just behind Frank on his left side, but gradually – very gradually – crept up until I was on the edge of the board, right next to him, where all the Winstons were kept.

A   [laughs] Frank loved his vegetables. That's what he called his cigarettes, by the way.

B   I stayed in our salad bar – I mean the control room – for awhile until I felt it was ok to go out in the studiowhen Frank started setting up for his "Son of Mr. Green Genes" guitar solo.

A   Yeah. I can never hear enough about Frank's guitar playing. Please, go on.

B   On pages 79 and 80, you can see Frank setting up the amplifiers in the studio. You'll need a more technical mind than mine to confirm the details, but if you look at the photos you can see there are two different amplifiers Frank had sequenced to give the sound of his Gibson an extraordinary texture. In fact, if you listen to it very carefully, there are parts when it seems like one guitar, and parts when it seems almost double-tracked.

A   And Frank set that up, I bet.

B   Methodically.

   The other thing about the "Son of" solo was that Frank played it in the control room, not the studio.

Ian piping it right.

"Son of" organ take.

Likin' it.

Listening back.

Acoustic in hand.

Working on "Peaches."

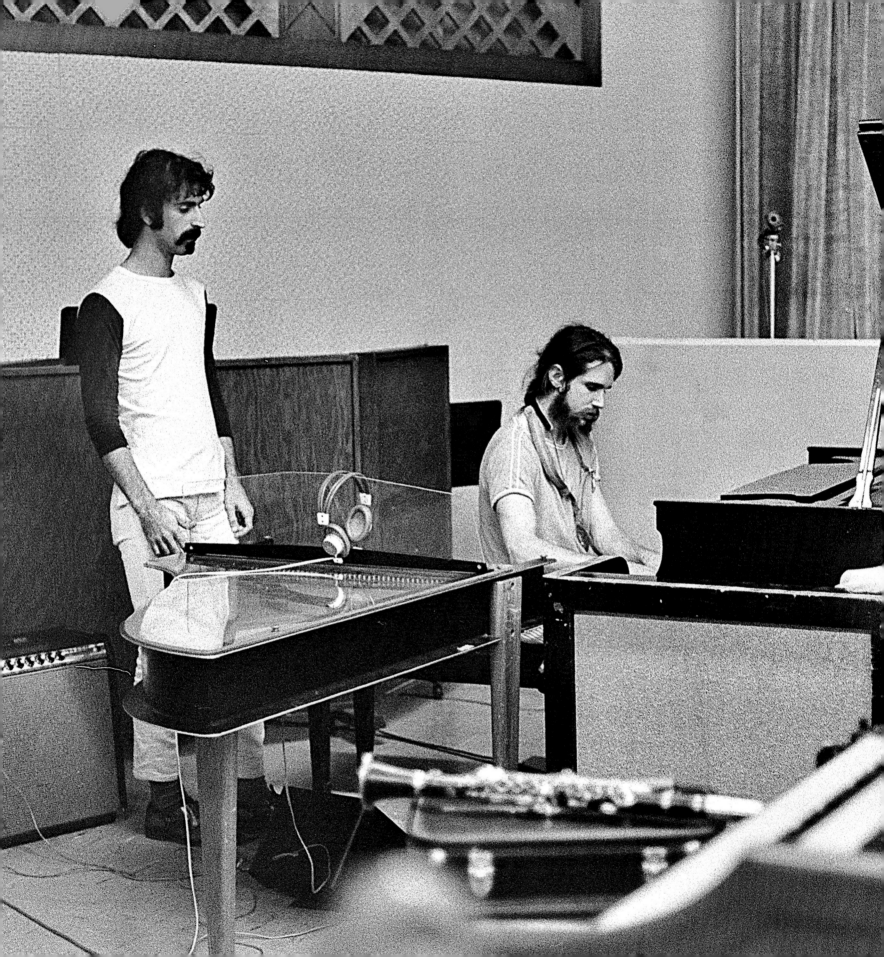

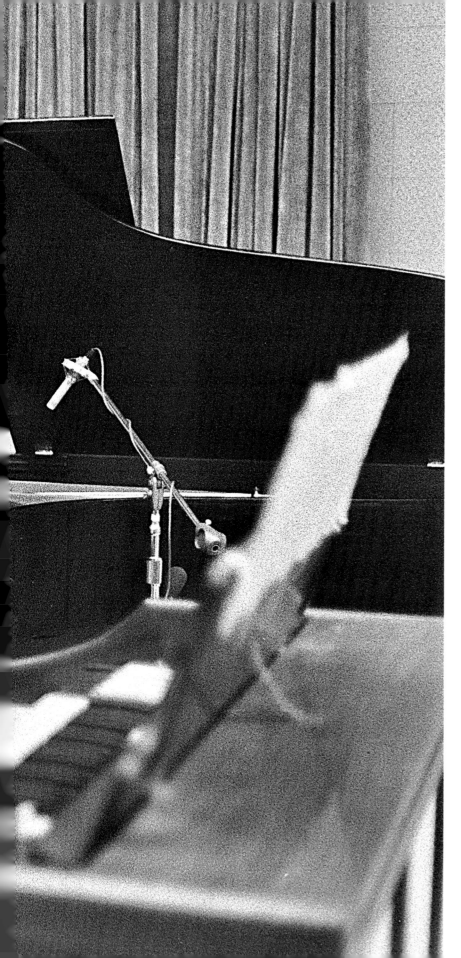

A Plugged directly into the board, right?

B   Yes.

Which was crazy for me, because here he was playing this great solo, and I was standing mere inches from him. In fact, the cover photo of *The Hot Rats Book* was taken just before he started the solo.

BTW, keeping all the *Hot Rats* negatives and transparencies safe and sound for nearly 50 years is an achievement I'm proud of, but there's one series of negatives that didn't make it through: The shots of the actual solo itself. So we scanned the original 1969 4x6 drug store prints of the solo and you can see them on pages 90 to 95. The shots are blurry because of the slow shutter speed, but they really capture the energy of the solo.

Every time I listen to it, it's hard to believe he was rocking out in the control room, in a very small space next to a bunch of tape machines rather than on a stage in front of 20,000 people. And he just made it up, on the spot, and I think each of the parts was done in one take.

A So great.

B   Here's the best part. You know at the very end of "Son of," when he takes the pick and runs it down the neck of his Gibson just before Ian does the final "dah-dah, dah-duh" on the piano?

A Of course.

B   I was sitting less than three feet from him when he did it.

A You're lucky the guitar string didn't snap and take out your eyes! But in all seriousness, that is the coolest thing that ever happened to you, right?

B   It was. But the reverie didn't last long, for it was quickly followed by one of the uncoolest things that ever happened to me.

So, yes, here I was, at the coolness pinnacle. I'd set a goal — a crazy, unachievable goal — to meet Frank Zappa — and achieved it beyond my wildest dreams. It was one of those "if they could only see me now" moments — at a *Hot Rats* session, next to Frank, all-access, blah, blah, blah.

Frank and Ian getting grand.

Grand 1.

Grand 2.

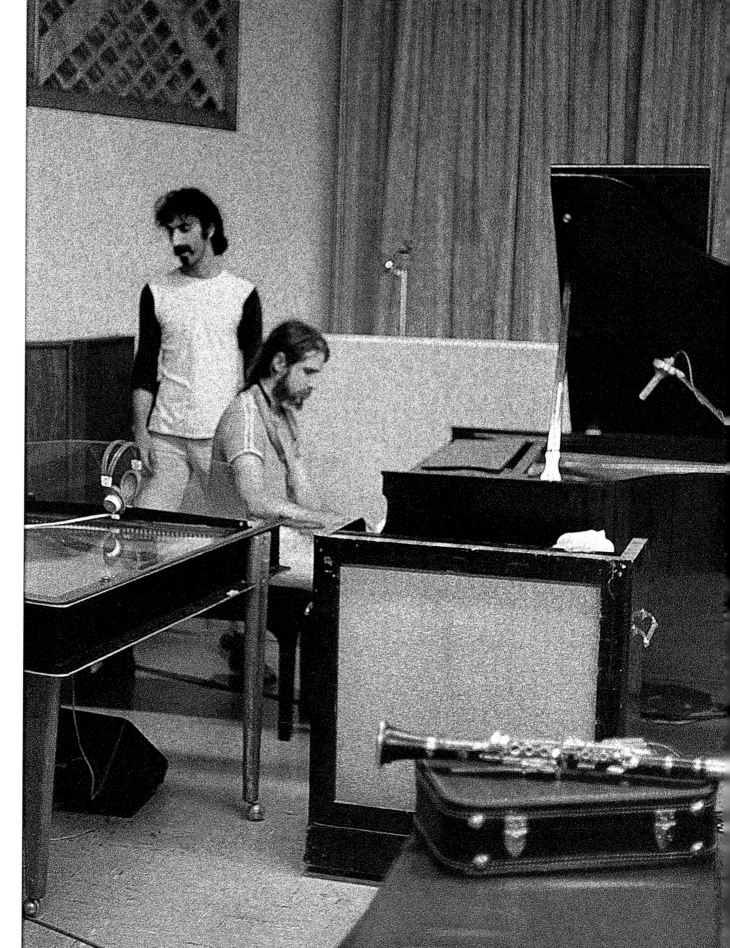

Grand 3.

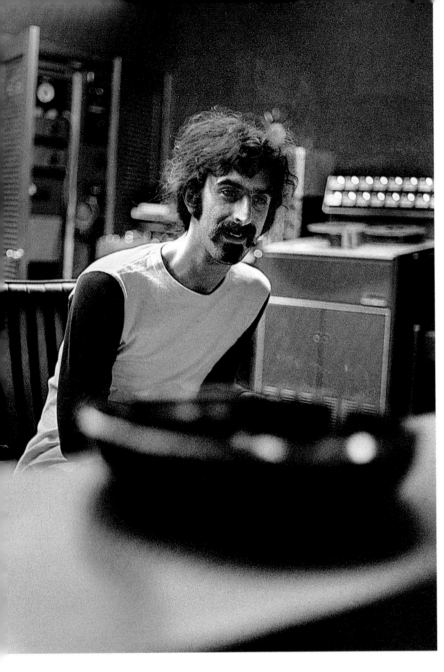

Tired "Camel."

The first *Hot Rats* session at Whitney was just over 12 hours long (7 PM to 7:30 AM) and significant portions of four tracks ("Peaches," "Green Genes," "Little Umbrellas," and "It Must Be a Camel") were recorded during it.

A   **In other words, you felt *the shit*. Go on . . .**

B   So it's around midnight and just as I started to relax a bit, I realized, with a sudden ferocity, that I was unbelievably hungry, famished in fact. And I had to get something to eat right *now*.

I turned to Frank and asked him if there was anywhere around the studio to get something to eat. He shook his head, then smiled and said the studio coffee machine had chicken soup.

A   **That sounds disgusting. Please don't tell me you ate chicken soup out of a coffee machine.**

B   Hang on, hang on. . . .

So I leave the control room and head out into mean, deserted halls of midnight Whitney. After grousing around, there it was, the enormous, battleship-esque, Whitney "coffee-machine-us maximus."

It had a single vertical column of buttons, each representing one variation of how people drink coffee. The top button was "Black," the next down was "Black with sugar," the next down was "Black with extra sugar" –

A   **I get the picture. [laughs]**

B   And sure enough, there, at the very bottom of this vertical column, was the last button, and it said –

A   **Chicken soup!**

B   Exactamundo. So I dropped my nickel or dime in, pressed the button, and down plopped a Dixie cup, followed by a puff of dusty chicken something, then a stream of *scalding-hot* water, which released all the artificial chicken *goodness* trapped within these misbegotten crystals.

Happy "Camel."

Dick and Frank making history.

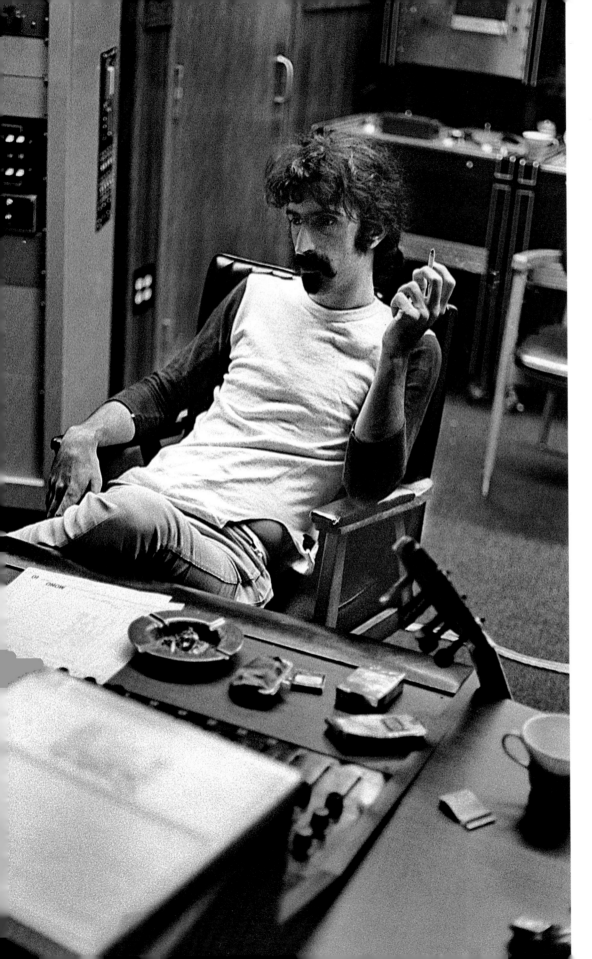

Needing something.

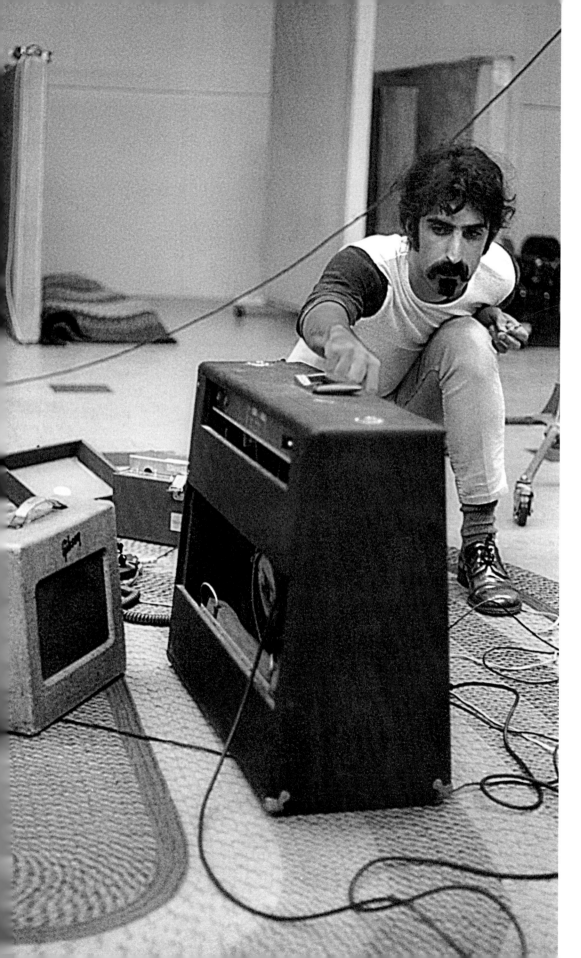

Getting the tone.

Tweaking the sound.

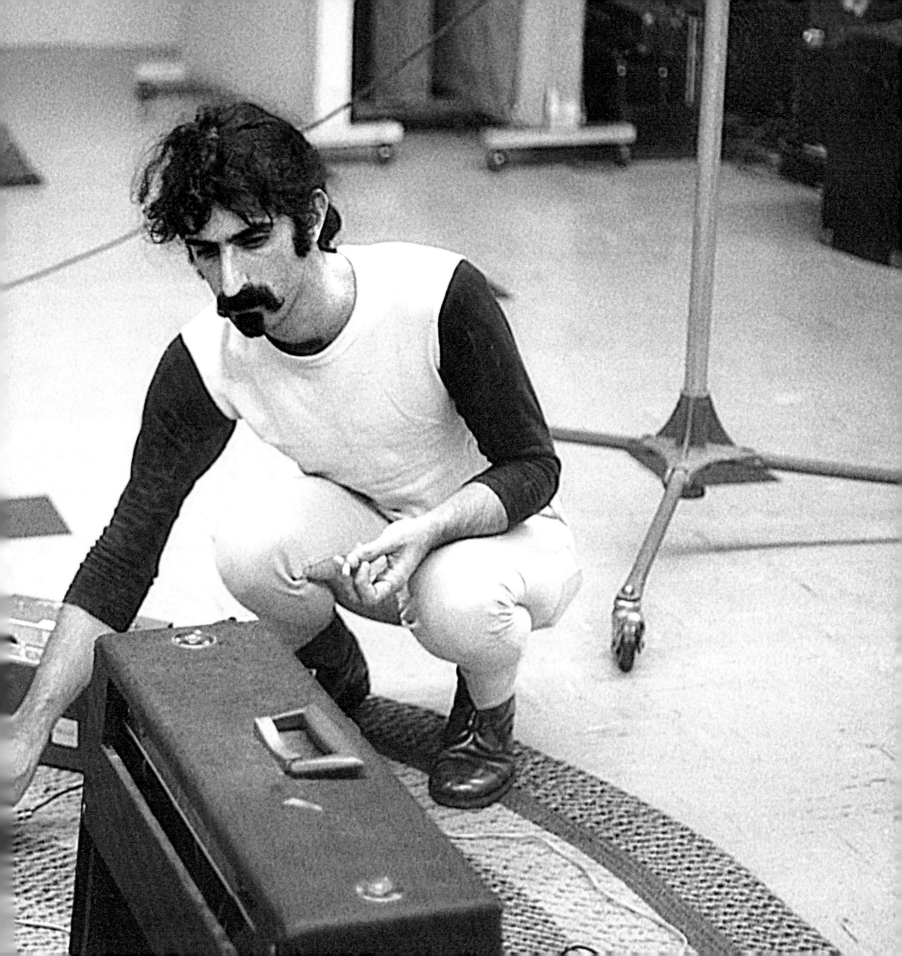

Dialing it in.

Practicing "Green Genes."

A   I'm surprised you didn't snort the chicken dust.

B   I should have.

Anyway, I walked back to the control room, my fingertips melting from the D-Cup heat, opened the door, walked in, and gently turned the broken-down Naugahyde chair so I could slowly accommodate myself down into its rickety seat. Of course, in doing so I emptied the soup all over my crotch, from which steam instantly emitted.

A   Ewwww.

B   That's *exactly* what your father said. He looked at me, smiled, and said, "Ewwww."

A   You got chicken dicked, Bro. So what did you do?

B   I played it cool, not much I could do, right? And, fortunately, those cast-iron Levis of the day saved me and the jewels from, uh, permanent damage.

So there I was, wearing wet Levi's with only seven more hours to go in the session.

A   That sounds terrible.

B   Oh, yeah.

A   [laughs] What was next?

B   Then Ian recorded all the horn parts to either "Peaches" or "Son of," which was very impressive.

A   How so?

B   He stood in the center of the studio, with a row of wind instruments – ranging from soprano sax to B-flat clarinet – beside him. He'd pick up one, say the alto sax, play the part, put it down, they'd rewind the 16-track, he'd pick up the next, maybe the tenor sax, play the part, put it down, they'd rewind the 16-track, then –

A   Rinse and repeat.

B   Exactly.

And my recollection – confirmed recently by Ian – was that he did many of the parts without a score, just doing the transpositions in his head.

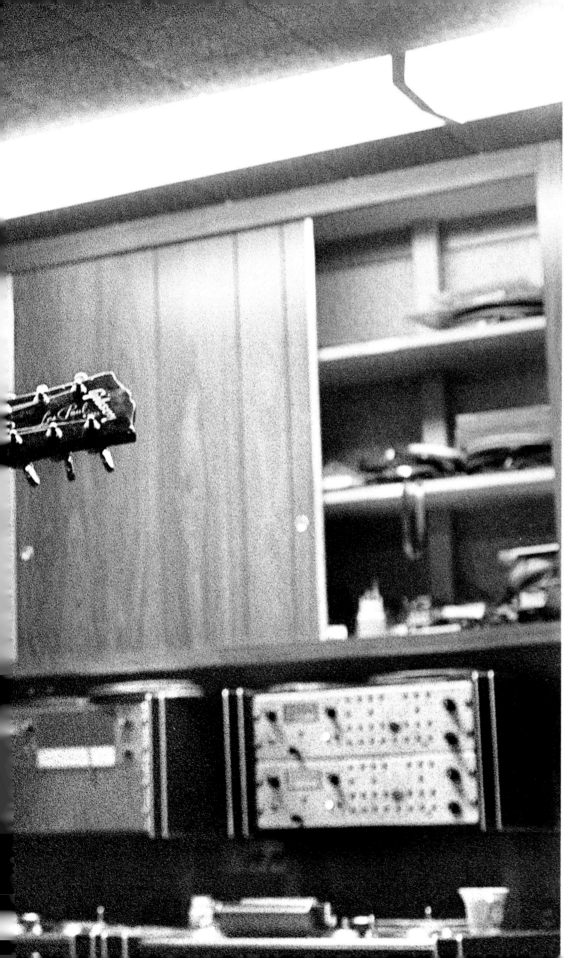

Getting "Green."

Frank in profile as he prepares to start the "Son of Mr. Green Genes" solo.

Getting more "Green."

A   I just gotta say, Ian is one incredible musician. I love that guy.

So the night's winding down.

B   Yes, and so was I. I think after "Peaches," they started on Ian's horn parts for either "Little Umbrellas" or "It Must Be a Camel," and then around 7:30, just as the 9-5ers were coming back, the session ended.

Not sure whether Carl Zappa came back to get us or whether Ian gave us a ride back, but by maybe 7:30 or 8 AM we were back home at Woodrow Wilson.

I think by that point I'd been up for something like 31 hours, so I was bush-wacked. But there was one detail left to be finalized: Where would I sleep? It was decided that the best place was on the floor of your purple living room, so Gail got me some sheets and a pillow and I was lights out.

AZ: What a day for little Bill!

Nailing "Son of Mr. Green Genes" solo.

Green Genes 1.

Green Genes 2.

Green Genes 3.

Green Genes 4.

Green Genes 5.

Green Genes 6.

Smoke 'em if you got 'em.

The extraordinary Ian Underwood.

Ian's "sucker" pants in the Whitney control room.

Practing "Peaches."

Laying down layers for "Peaches."

Feedback from Frank.

Louder in the cans.

More sax with Dick on "Peaches."

105

Sax break.

Happy playback.

On to the B-flat bass clarinet.

Job well done nap.

AN ANGELIC HARP, THE **SESSION** 2 BREAKUP PRESS RELEASE, AND A SHAGGY SUNSET STROLL. YUP, JUST ANOTHER 1969 DAY WITH FRANK ZAPPA.

Frank commanding the Sunset board.

Playing it back.

A   So did you sleep for like a billion hours?

B   Yup, I think I woke up around 1. And I don't care who knows it!

A   So what's happening in the house?

B   I have a confession to make.

A   What? Is this where you admit to me you're secrectly a werewolf?

B   No, nothing like that, but here it is. I didn't take any notes during my visit. So I know *what* happened, but I'm not sure *when* – as in what exact *day* – it did. The studio stuff, that's pretty easy, we got that straight, but the rest of it, as in what happened the second day versus the third . . .

A   I think you're being too hard on yourself. But if you think it'll help, I could always punch your face in with some salad tongs to see if it jogs any memories. Or we could just carry on . . .

B   Tempting, but, ok, let's carry on.

So I get up knowing that the session tonight will start at 7 at the legendary Sunset Sound, so I don't have a whole lot of time on my hands, plus, there are some very interesting things brewing in the Basement.

But first, I have a problem to deal with.

A   What . . .?

B   Sometime while I was asleep, one or more of the many, many Zappa cats used my precious suitcase – that had been left wide open by its idiot owner – as a litter box.

A   I'm not surprised. The cats in our house growing up were piss ninjas.

B   So the first thing I had to do was find your mother and see if I might get some clothes washed. I was desperately trying not to be a nuisance – especially since she was within days of giving birth to Dweezil – but she was very kind, washed them for me, and left them folded on the dining room table.

So, then I go down to the basement and start the day with a cold Pepsi and a couple of smokes, and Frank joins me shortly thereafter.

There was an electric typewriter on his work table, and he starts some serious typing.

And, much to my surprise, began telling me about it.

A   What was he working on?

B   A draft of the Mothers breakup press release, which he let me read, and which I later surreptitiously photographed when no one was looking.

A   Get the fuck out of here! That's heavy.

B   It was the only – and I do mean only – boundary-crossing thing I did while I was there. I knew it was a historical document of sorts and felt it should be saved for posterity.

A   It's cool, I'm glad we have it.

B   Whew – I'm relieved.

Here's where it gets crazy, because Frank not only let me read the damn thing, but kinda asked what I thought of it.

A   So what did you say?

B   I don't remember, but I'm sure I *didn't* say, "Goddamn it, Frank, what in the name of Anton Webern are you thinking!?" and rip it up in his face.

A   If you'd have done that, he might have salad-tonged you.

B   Oh no! . . . But then things got really interesting because maybe around three or so, Herb Cohen shows up.

But before we get into the details about Frank's press-release discussion with Herb, this reminds me of something I want to say about your father, if I may.

A   Shoot.

B   As you might imagine, I have humble-bragged about my time with him for 50 years. And, for those who are interested, my answer to the "What was Frank Zappa like?" question is very simple.

I always say, "Frank Zappa was the politest person I've ever met." And I've met my fair share of people, and he's at the top of the list.

Cookie Banana Underwood.

After digesting the press release, staring at the session sheets, Don Preston's new realty.

I have decided to disband the group as a performing entity. It is still possible we might get together occasionally to record. It is also possible we will reorganize as a group for a featured appearance in Uncle Meat.

I have decided to disband for these reasons:

1. It is unethical to ask you all to wait around for some potential gold mine in the future while many of you have wives & children to support. If I disband the group you are free to join other groups, seek other employment, and thereby achieve some sort of economic stability again.

2. There is no hope America will ever really prefer our music to the offerings of the more commercial groups. If we cannot command top prices for concert bookings, it is useless to perform. Every tour we ever made has come out in the red. ████████████████████████████

3. I wanted the group to be a frightening big band. A group that could play anything better than anybody, do theatrical absurdities & deliver a worthwhile message to an audience that really needs to hear it. The only thing frightening about the band today is the expenses, the wrong notes & disinterested performances, and the inability of the audience to grasp what the group is really doing. Rather than fire some members of the group (which would alter the electro-chemical personality balance considerably) and try to continue on with this tragic program, I felt it would be more honest to say: "THE MOTHERS DIDN'T REALLY MAKE IT & I'M STUPID FOR EXPECTING SO MUCH." ████████████████████████████████████

Mothers breakup press release draft.

A   So you think he wouldn't have salad-tonged you, is that what you're saying?

B   No. I don't think he would have. From what I saw, Frank treated everyone, no matter what their status or station, with the same dignity and respect.

I bring this up now because I can clearly recall how he introduced me when Herb came in. I was sitting on the sofa and here comes Herb, his manager and *partner* –

A   Partner who totally fucked my dad over. Not a fan of that guy. Go on . . .

B   OK. And then Frank goes out of his way to introduce me, tells Herb where I'm from, what I'm doing there, on and on, which he clearly didn't have to do, nor did I expect him to, nor would I have been offended in the least if he didn't.

I mean, I was some random kid, sitting on the sofa, reading an old interview he did in *Hit Parader* magazine or something – I'm sure there were always people like me on the periphery like that – and for him to go out of his way like he did. . . . It was cool, very cool.

A   I know. Frank was fucking cool. I'm marveling at what you are talking about.

B   So Herb comes in and is trying to talk Frank out of sending the release he's written, to which Frank responds, with great passion – and I can still hear him saying it: "I don't want to put out another *fraudulent* record company press release."

A   Dude, the feeling in the room must have been gnarly.

B   Yes it was.

At some point Herb realized this and then, very politely, asked me if he could "speak to Frank in private" or something like that, and I went outside and hung out with Moon and Carl.

Herb was gone when I came back and things were cool.

Then, as every day I was there, around 5:30 or 6, plates of well-proportioned and excellently prepared food would magically appear. I still remember Frank and Gail's generous hospitality.

A   One of the things I miss most in life is having dinner with

Frank in the live room with Sunset Sound engineer, Brian Ingoldsby.

my parents. So it's really nice to reminisce about things like this with you, Bill.

So what did you do next?

B   We left for Sunset Sound.

Where Whitney was out of the way and isolated, Sunset Sound was: 1. One of the most famous recording studios in the world and 2. In the midst of the insane summer-of-'69 vibrancy of Sunset Strip. So, while I'd gotten comfortable at the house and at Whitney, just seeing the hordes of rock 'n' roll people with their shags and snakeskin boots as we drove down Sunset . . . I had to admit, again, I was out of my league.

A reality reinforced when we got to Sunset, which was clearly hallowed ground.

And, for some reason, Dick Kunc either didn't – or couldn't – make the session that night, so our engineer was a guy named Brian Ingoldsby.

And, they hadn't finished striking the previous session, so there was this enormous harp in the middle of the studio, that Frank began noodling with, and was cool with me shooting him as he did.

A   **Was he as good on the harp as he was on the guitar?**

B   Not that I could make out. But it was fascinating to hear him play around with it, the Zappa mind at work.

What I should have said – and it came to me just the other day, almost 50 years late – what I *should* have said while he was at the harp was: "Hey, Frank, can you play 'Louie, Louie' on that?

A   **If you did say that back then it would have gone one of two ways: 1. That could have been the most embarrassing and lame moment for you or 2. He probably would have laughed.**

B   Or, laughed as he applied the tongs . . .

But I must say, for the record, Frank did not play the harp on *Hot Rats*. Other than that, I don't remember much about the Sunset session, simply cause I got bounced out almost before it started.

A   **This is a record scratch moment. Who bounced you out?**

B   No one directly asked me to leave, but when Mothers keyboardist Don Preston arrived, things got a tad uncomfortable.

A   **What happened?**

B   It had something to do with the breakup of the Mothers and beyond that I don't know. I got two shots off before realizing – and it was very clear – that Don wasn't a happy camper. He might have even given me the evil eye, so I thought it best to make myself scarce.

A   **What did you do?**

B   This Buckeye Nerd, no matter how outclassed, eagerly ventured into the buzz of a hot, late-summer night on the snakeskin sidewalks of the shag-haired Sunset Strip.

A   **I gather you felt very out of place?**

B   And then some. It was strange, very strange.

And when I got back to the studio – maybe an hour-and-a-half later – Don was gone and the session was almost over. So not as many photos of this one as the others.

A   **Then you headed back to Woodrow Wilson?**

B   Yes, and, after maybe an hour or two in the basement, I hit that great purple-living-room floor . . .

Acoustic experments.

Harp infatuation experimentation 1.

Harp infatuation experimentation 2.

Harp infatuation experimentation 3.

Last, for the record,
despite these photos,
Frank did not—
I repeat,
did not—play the harp
on *Hot Rats*.
Nor, for that matter,
did anyone else.
Thank you.

Zappa in the Woodrow Wilson basement
with his Scully.

A   Ok, you wake up and it's a new day in Zappa world. What kind of insanity was going on?

B   Well it was different because there was no session, which simplified things considerably. I'm also realizing I have only three days left, so I'm trying to make the most of them.

So I take my usual spot, in the center of the sofa, studying every piece of Zappa ephemera I can get my hands on while Frank works at his work table.

A   Just the two of you?

B   Mostly, yes. Gail might come down with Moon for awhile, or Moon might wander down on her own, Janet was in and out, Kansas was doing things but, for the most part, it was just the two of us.

A   Did you talk?

B   Some, but I was pretty careful not to bug him, though if I ran across something interesting, I'd ask him about it.

A   Example, please.

B   One of the clippings that blew my mind was finding out he was on *The Steve Allen Show* playing a bike as a musical instrument in the early '60s, way before the Mothers.

So, I'd just call out, "Hey Frank, how'd you get on *The Steve Allen Show*?" He'd tell me the story, I might ask a few follow-up questions, then he'd go back to work, and I'd go back to ephemera hunting. I also remember asking him a lot of questions about Ronnie and Kenny Williams, who were the subjects of a couple of songs on *We're Only In It For The Money*.

He was also great with technical stuff, which I also asked him about. An example, and I'm not sure how it came up, but we were talking about the covers of *We're Only In It For The Money* and *Sgt. Pepper* and he went into great detail about how the two covers were done, how all the people on the Beatles cover were blown up life-size so there was just one photo but all the background people on *Money* were individually stripped in at the printer, things like that.

This might be off topic, but it's worth noting his general knowledge was both wide and deep, especially about anything remotely related to any form of media — TV, film, print, recording — as well as everything related to the music business. You got the feeling of tremendous overall competence with Frank, and I've no doubt he was as good with a soldering gun as a guitar pick.

I've always been a big Stanley Kubrick fan and the descriptions of Stanley's obsession with all the details of cameras, lenses, and the pica-widths of *Clockwork Orange* newspaper ads in India, remind me a lot of Frank.

In short: he loved to know how things worked.

Sorry, I've gone off on a tangent. So here we are, hanging in the basement, and there's a knock on the double doors, they open, the sunlight streams in, and — abba zaba! — it's Captain Beefheart and Magic Band member Zoot Horn Rollo (real name: Bill Harkelroad, and the Captain's was Don Van Vliet, of course). They were in the neighborhood, and just popped in.

Frank was glad to see them, stopped what he was doing, and they hung out for maybe 30 minutes or so, with me on the perimeter.

A   OMG! You got to hang with the Captain! That must have been awesome.

B   Yes! First of all, I was a huge *Trout Mask Replica* fan so it was fantastic. But Don was the polar opposite of Frank in almost every way: where Frank wanted to make everyone comfortable, I got the sense that Don liked to make people uncomfortable. If you asked Frank a question, you got a straight answer; if you gave Don the answer, he might ask you a straight question.

Plus, Don was a big guy. I'm guessing over 6'2," easy, and was built like a damn linebacker, so if he wanted to weird you out, I'm sure he could. And he had a very, very big head.

Bill was also very tall, maybe 6'4" or 6'5," reed thin, and had incredibly long hair.

And Don looked different from *Trout Mask Replica* because he had this big Van Dyke moustache. And kept asking me what I thought of it. He'd even get right in my face, and say, "Whattaya think? You like it? You like it? Whattaya think?" as he twirled his moustache.

A   He gave you the full Captain treatment. He got all up in your grill. Did you guys touch noses?

A CAPTAIN BEEFHEART POP-IN AND A PRIVATE FRANK ZAPPA CONCERT.

B   Wish we had – and that I'd honked his nose with your salad tongs.

But it was ok, he knew I was a fan and was just doing a focus group, I guess. But it highlighted the differences between the two: I can't imagine Frank asking anyone – let alone someone like me – what they thought about anything of his, or giving a shit about what they said. Don, it was clear, was constantly seeking affirmation.

So they shot the breeze, Bill told some very funny stories about dealing with his draft board, then they left and Frank went back to work.

Around six the plates of food magically appeared and then Frank spent the evening editing "Peaches en Regalia" on his two-track Scully.

Which was another mind-blowing experience in and of itself.

Let's start here: The original "Peaches" track was at least twice as long – maybe more – than the 3:38 version on *Hot Rats*. I remember listening to the album when it came out and I was surprised at how radically "Peaches" had been edited.

Frank did all the editing of the two-track "Peaches" master sitting, for hours, and hours, in one of the most uncomfortable chairs of all time (I know, I sat in it). You can see it in the photos, how hunched over the guy is – it hurts your damn back just to look at it! Plus, check him out slaving over the Scully, hell, Ahmet, he can't even fit his legs under the damn thing.

And, he doesn't even have a table to put the take-up reels on – he has to hold them in his lap.

A   It's unbelievable.

B   So I sat – at a safe distance – and just marveled – marveled – at how gracefully he did it. And listen to "Peaches" on headphones sometime, I'm guessing there are a least 20 edits – maybe as many as 40! – and if you can hear any of 'em . . . You're lyin', cause you can't.

A   Frank was an absolute mutant with bat-like hearing. He was an alien.

B   If everything I just talked about wasn't enough, all I wish was that every Zappa fan would have been with me to bear witness to what happened next.

So the night's winding down, it's maybe two or three in the morning, just the two of us, Frank's puttering around, I'm ephemera diving, not much is being said, which is ok, no problem.

As I mentioned earlier, there is a row of pretty big amplifiers on the wall opposite the couch. So Frank walks in with his Gibson and plugs it into one of the amplifiers. Now remember, I'd never even seen him holding a guitar down there, let alone playing one.

Then he turns to me and says – with complete seriousness – "Do you mind if I play my guitar for awhile?"

A   [laughs] Wow.

B   Of course I say, "Of course not."

Then he begins what I can only describe as a 20-minute solo guitar concert. He's standing there playing away, incredible melodies coming out, then he'd go to something more bluesy, then more rock. He'd go from loud to quiet, then back again.

It was as if he were burning off excess energy, exploring new musical ideas, and having one helluva good time – simultaneously.

Ahmet, you might have heard this every day, but to experience it even once – incredible, simply incredible.

A   I think I know how you felt 'cause I have been in awe of Frank's guitar playing my whole life. So did you just sit there soaking it all in?

B   It was awkward at first, because I didn't want to sit and stare, because it certainly wasn't being played for my benefit, so I'd read something, kinda peek out and watch, then go back to reading, then peek and watch.

Then, after about 20-minutes it was over. And we both called it a day.

Scully surgery.

Puff fatigue.

Slices of "Peaches" on the floor.

Sounding good.

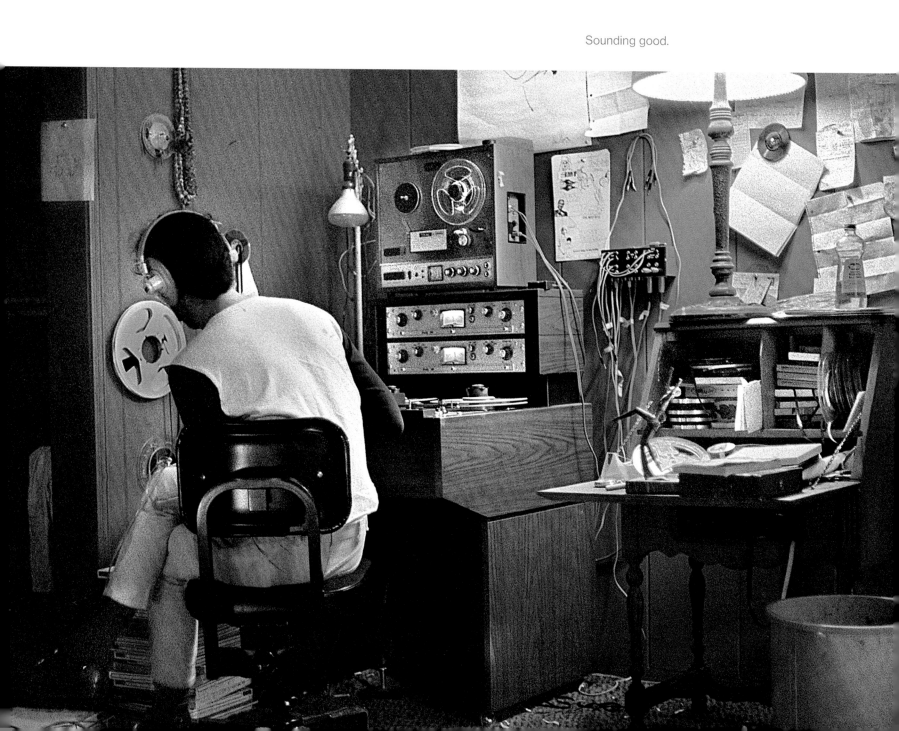

LAST NIGHT AT WHITNEY AND THE TALE OF THE MYSTERY BABYSITTER.

SESSION 3

A   Session Three. Go.

B   Somebody drove us to Whitney around 6:30, and, when we arrived, there was this strange guy sitting in the back of the control room. He was maybe 50-60, and was dressed so, to use the term of the day, "square," I wondered if my parents had sent one of their friends to check up on me. He was friendly, seemed like Frank knew him.

A   Who was he?

B   Hang on, because first I gotta tell you how he helped me get one of the best shots of the visit.

A   Which shot was that?

B   The shot of Frank looking off to the upper left as he touches his moustache. (See photo on page 151.)

My point here is not photographic technique, but to point out for the "what-was-Frank-Zappa-really-like?" fans out there one of his most endearing skills: He was an unbelievable listener.

A   He sure was.

B   So this guy was making small talk to Frank, who, as you can see by the picture, was listening to the guy with great intensity.

My experience, admittedly limited, was that, when Frank was listening to you, you were the only person who existed.

He was listening to this guy so intently he didn't notice I was taking the shot.

Zappa with his 16-track tapes.

A   **Bill, enough. Who the fuck was he?**

B   Ok fine I'll tell you. The mystery man gets up to go to the bathroom or something and I ask Frank, "Uh, who is this guy?" And Frank says, with a smile, "He's the babysitter from the Mormon Church."

A   **What?**

B   Since Whitney was owned by the Church, they sent somebody over to check things out. Maybe to make sure , I dunno, that Frank wasn't recording something in a minor key or something.

    But the four of us were clearly well-behaved citizens who probably would have emptied all the ashtrays before we left if they'd have asked us, so there really wasn't much to be worried about.

A   **Well one of the best Mormon Church experiences I ever had was being in the same room as Donny Osmond and Frank as they talked about the Mormon faith. But that's a story for a different book.**

    So what was happening at the session?

B   It was another Ian night where he did a ton of wind and keyboard work on "Peaches," "Son of," "Umbrellas," and "Camel."

A   **Maybe we should have hit this earlier, but you've never mentioned two of the *Hot Rats* songs, "Willie the Pimp" and "Gumbo Variations." Anything on those recorded while you were there?**

B   No, unfortunately. The first time I heard them was the first time I heard the record itself. "Gumbo" is a favorite, I could listen to Ian's sax solo all day, every day.

A   **Anything else interesting?**

B   Well, as I look back on the photos, one of the things that continues to amaze me, especially given my own production experiences, is just how damn smoothly everything went, how seemingly effortlessly it all came together.

A His work ethic and creativity knew no bounds

B Yes

As I look back, I think, wait a minute, Frank wrote all the scores, arranged all the scores – including for the at-least-13 instruments Ian played on "Peaches" and probably the same number on "Son of" – produced the record – which meant booking the studio time, making sure the people and instruments were all there – among three different studios, all over L.A., BTW – he directed the engineering of the record – including detailed microphone placement – and he mixed it.. And, finally, right before my very eyes, he edited the whole damn thing – in his basement!

And did so under a pretty tight deadline – a really tight deadline, in fact – because the finished record was in my hands less than six weeks from the last session.

A   Like I said, he was an alien. His work ethic and creativity knew no bounds.

B   Yes. And with one small exception I'll mention shortly, there was never a single moment where you felt Frank was under any kind of pressure or that anyone else was either.

So to the long list of your father's "core skills," as someone in HR might put it, let's add "project management" to the list.

A   So what was the exception?

B   You can see it in one of the photos from the back of the control room where Frank and Dick are in the foreground and Ian is playing out in the studio. I think they were doing "punch-ins" and Frank was getting frustrated that Dick wasn't punching in on cue.

A   A great photo, I like how Frank's pointing at Dick who's holding up his hands, like, "I'm doing the best I can."

B   [laughs] Exactly.

But other than that – which was very was very mild as these things go – all three sessions were totally stress free.

A   But go back. You forgot something pretty big about all the things he did on the album?

B   What?

A   He played on it like a motherfucker.

B   Damn! How could I possibly forget. And several *great* solos.

A   And I'll give you something else, too.

B   Tell me.

A   He designed the album cover and packaging.

B   [Head-slapping sound]] Damn! Which is where the whole thing started: the cover design.

I've always felt the totality of what he did has never been properly appreciated, let alone analyzed or understood.

A   I can't argue you with you.

B   Back to the studio. It was another all nighter and then Ian, I think, gave us a ride home and that was it.

A   So goodnight everybody –

B   From the Purple Bedroom on Woodrow Wilson Drive.

A   [laughs]

Ian nailing "Little Umbrellas."

Ian at the Hammond organ with an engineerd cardboard music stand attachment.

Underwood figuring it out.

Frank to the rescue.

Play this right.

The masters.

Frank playing his Hofner Bass.

Using the bass as a sonic tool to simulate orchestral instruments as overdubs using VSO (varispeed oscillator) tape machine techniques.

Adding even more layers to "Peaches."

149

Flutes and tapes.

What part do I work on next?

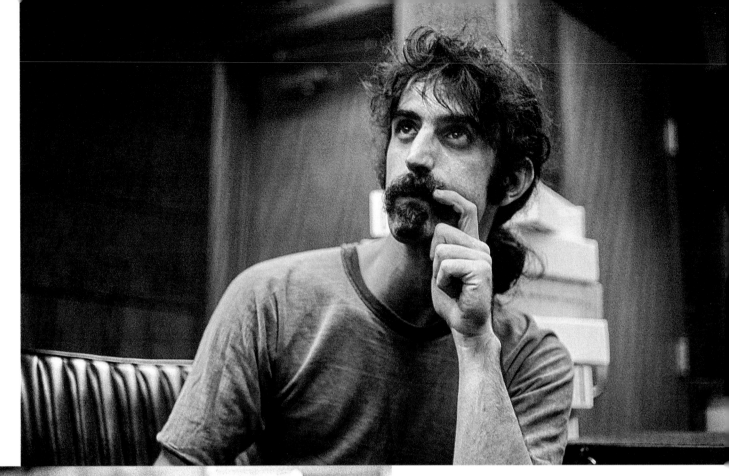

Listening to the
mystery Babysitter.

At the board, starting another
round of horn parts.

153

Ian on soprano sax.

155

Adjusting those nobs and faders.

Chewin' smoke.

Frustrations with Dick.

Hot Rats happiness.

"Let's

do

one

of

those

camera-in-the-mirror

dealies."

FLY HOME SLOW.
THE JOURNEY ENDS, WITH A SELFIE.

A   It's your last day in L.A. Any more cat piss that you had to deal with? What are your final memories?

B   [Laughs] No more cat piss, thank god, but, to fully set the context, I believe it was a Saturday, and my flight back left early Sunday morning, maybe eight-ish, so I basically had 24 hours left.

Given that, I have only two clear memories of the last day, as crazy as it might sound.

The first is getting a reluctant, *reluctant* Janet Ferguson to drive me out to get some beer. I had to cajole her to make a beer run with me, which was no easy task.

A   Why?

B   Well, first of all, Janet regarded me, perhaps correctly, given our mutual standings in the universe at that moment, as a lower life form. But since there was no one else there to ask . . .

So she drove me to the closest store that sold beer, which might have been the legendary Canyon Country Store on Laurel Canyon Boulevard. She also probably had to actually *buy* me the beer because I wasn't 21 yet, so maybe her annoyance was justified. I just remember trying to make small talk in the car, and every new effort was lamer than the previous — I might have even asked her what she wanted Santa Claus to bring her for Christmas, I dunno. But whatever I tried, it was uncool, for sure.

A   [laughs] Don't take this the wrong way, but yeah, you sound like a tough hang. And I love you Bill, but seriously, you had no game.

B   [Laughs] I was a late bloomer, what can I say?

The other was the early evening visit from Gail's mother, Mrs. Sloatman —

A   Her name was Laura, but we called her Tutu.

B   Ok. So Tutu and a male friend came over that night, just to hang out for a bit before they went to dinner. They were both straight-looking and the conversation was very casual, and Frank was most respectful, if not deferential, to Tutu and her friend.

Frank graciously introduced me, I hung around for a bit, on the periphery, of course, then probably went outside to stare at the stars or something.

A   And the rest of the night?

B   The rest of the night was like the other nights: He worked, I read and looked around, asked questions if any came to me, and that was it.

A   Just the two of you again?

B   Yep. I hung with him, all night.

Then, around five Sunday morning, I asked him if he had a *Yellow Pages* for me to call a cab. And I think he went ahead and called it for me himself.

A   That was nice of him.

B   So he worked and I waited — I can still remember how the blue early morning light looked out of the basement door. But I had one last mission, left, and it was a big one.

A   Tell me.

B   Well, I'd fastidiously avoided anything that would seem self-serving while I was there, but I couldn't leave without asking him if we could have our picture taken together. And he responded positively, and, grasping that there was nobody else there, he had the perfect solution.

A   What was it?

B   He said, and I can still hear him saying it, "Let's do one of those camera-in-the-mirror dealies" and, since the closest mirror was in the bathroom down there, we walked in, stood in front of the mirror, I held the Nikkormat up, and fired my last three shots. And prayed one of them had us both in it, was properly exposed (the bathroom had just a single ceiling fixture, not the best lighting), and given the slow shutter speed (probably a 1/30th or a 1/15th of a second), we weren't blurry all over the place.

Then that was it, and, as if on cue, the cab arrived, I said goodbye, dragged my Sam — suitcase out the door, and headed to LAX to catch my plane home.

Frank Zappa & Bill Gubbins.
"Camera-in-the-mirror dealie"

A

All these pictures of Frank have remained unseen until now.

CODA
LIFE AFTER Z.
A QUICK LOOK BACK
ON 50 YEARS
OF
HUMBLE-BRAGGING.

B   The flight back was uneventful and Dave Kresak picked me up at the Toledo airport – in the Polara, of course – and immediately asked me why I was talking so funny. Which I was, because I'd picked up some of Frank's speech mannerisms.

Next I had to figure out where to have the precious film developed. It didn't take me long to find the very, very best place in Bowling Green: a drug store. It was a place called Roger's Drug and since it was right by the railroad tracks that ran through the center of town, its slogan was, "By the tracks."

So I dropped the film off, and when I got them back, to my shock, they weren't too bad.

A   **Dude, they're fucking awesome.**
B   Why thank you, Ahmet, that means a great deal to me. They were cool to have – I was able to whip them out at any occasion where I thought someone might get a kick out of them, or be impressed by them. Which, as I quickly found out, wasn't as often as I thought. Sometime in 1970, I did send the proof sheets to *Rolling Stone*, and was surprised to get a note back saying they wanted a print of the one of him playing the harp, which I sent, and they ran it twice, once in 1970 for a "Random Notes" item and once in 1971 for their Lester Bangs' review of *Chunga's Revenge*. I think I was paid $25.00 each for usage – and they spelled my name correctly only once. Which is par for the course, I had a photo published in the *New York Times* in the late '90s and even the *Times* mangled my name.

But I was never going to be a professional photographer, so it wasn't a big deal. I made my mind up early on I wanted to be an editor, not a writer or a photographer.

A   **Did you ever see Frank again or talk to him?**
B   I sent sent him a thank-you note after my visit and asked him what it would take to have him give a lecture and show his *Burnt Weeny Sandwich* film at a Bowling Green student film society I'd started called Middle Class Youth (a name Frank liked, which isn't surprising because it was certainly inspired by his naming methodology).

I saw him two other times. The first was after a show in Columbus, Ohio in '73, I think. I gave my name to someone backstage and, low and behold, he remembered me, brought me back, we said hello and he even invited me to join him at breakfast the next morning. I sat at a table with Frank, Howard Kaylan and a friend of mine named Bil Murray.

Then once more, in 1974, I interviewed him in Toledo, Ohio, for *Exit*, a local magazine I was managing editor of, an interview that's still floating around on the Internet.

A   **And that was it. No further contact.**
B   None.

And, for over 45 years the negatives and slides sat in a musty filing cabinet, until I put them in a safe-deposit box when I moved to Nashville. All these pictures of Frank have remained unseen until now.

A   **That is so nuts! What a bizarre tale. You and Frank look so young in the "camera-in-the-mirror dealies" photo. That shot really gets me emotional. You know Bill, you're an artist in your own right and what you've done is extraordinary. I'm so glad we met and I wanna thank you so much for your memories, these spectacular images and for traveling us all back through time. And even though you're not a werewolf or fish mutant, you really are a damn interesting human being.**

I'm sure Frank thought the same.

!

Ahmet Zappa is an entertainer, *New York Times* Best Selling Author, film and television screenwriter, director, producer, inventor, futurist and radio personality. He's also acted in feature films and TV, and hosted hundreds of hours of television. Additionally he runs the extensive Frank Zappa estate through the Zappa Trust as co-Trustee. Most importantly he is a proud husband and father of two.

Bill Gubbins has had a distinguished publishing and media career, including editing national magazines like *Creem*, *Moviegoer*, and *Country Weekly*. While at Whittle Communications, he was a founder of *Channel One*, the Peabody Award winning in-school newscast. He currently operates Gubbins Light & Power Company, a firm creating custom media properties for clients such as T-Mobile, Microsoft, and Red Robin restaurants. His photographs have been published in the *New York Times* and *Rolling Stone*, and been exhibited in the U.S. and Europe.

ACKNOWLEDGMENTS

Ahmet

This book is dedicated to Shana, Halo and Arrow. You're my everything.

Special thanks to: My Zappas, My Muldoons, Melanie Starks, Joe Travers, Mike Mesker, Holland Greco, Erin Weiss, Billy Bob Thornton, Andee Nathanson and John Cerullo

The Rocktails Team: Richard Scheltinga & Brendan Smith

And last, but not least, Bill Gubbins

Bill

Dedication
Mary Lynn Schaefer
William & Marjorie Gubbins
Nita Beth Moore, Robert Talbert

If Not For You . . .
Ahmet Zappa, John Cerullo, Mike Fink, Melanie Starks
Denny Post, Terry Hummel
Charlie & Bernita Moore
Frank & Gail Zappa
Tom Jacobs (1950-2018)

Essential Ingredients
Steven Friedlander, Andrew Greenaway,
Glenn Blake, Dr. James Farrell, Larry Hageman,
Billy Bob Thornton
David Kresak

Nos Paenitet Me Daturam
Brett Clement, Mick Ekers, Chanan Haspal,
John Marks, James Richardson, Calvin Schenkel,
Charles Ulrich, Ian Underwood, Steve Vai,
Danny Wilson

Ashley Capps, Michael Cuscuna, Cat Kahnle,
Nicole Kopperud, Paul Krassner, Andee Nathanson,
Gary Panter, Jean-Luc Ponty, Jim Ritts,
Fred Seibert, Kevin Stein

Five-Star Yelp Reviews To
The Scans-I: Steve Rifkin, Nicholas Xavier Esposito
(Hank's Photographic Services Inc., Mt. Vernon, NY);
Production: Clare Cerullo; The Scans-II:
Vicki Moore (Chromatics, Nashville, TN); Financial
Guidance: Jesse Hammond (CPA, Knoxville, TN),
Gary Dover (CPA, Nashville, TN);
Fine Dining: Sam B's (Bowling Green, OH)

Primary Caregivers
Billy Altman, Joe Bernard, Tim Brown, Scott Colthorp,
Richard & Gina Curtis, Charlie DeBevoise,
Scott Eyman, Mark Goldman, Scott Helbing,
Bill King, Tony Kiser, Ellen Knisley, Tom Lombardo,
Candy Maldonado, Keith Miles, Bil Murray,
Mark Scheerer, Denise Stevens,
Mark & Abby Werder, Ed Winter

Sam & Kathy Cercone, Scott Colby, Frank Finn,
Steve Goodwin & Mary Winner,
Charlie "Cuckoo" Jamieson, Robert Jamieson,
Steve Lomas, Tom Martin, Dan Medsker,
Norm Pearlstine, Jeffrey Plansker, Rand Russell

Eternal Father, Strong To Save
Bill Burkart, Gerald Dillingham, Joe Dondanville,
Alan Greenberg, Jim Hilmer, Rob Lundgren,
Andrea Mayfield, Alan Powell, Lynda Weinman,
Chris Whittle

Kurt Andersen, Lisa Atkin, Linda Ayles-Johnson & Brad
Johnson, Lester Bangs, Liz Mynko Bartell, Frenchy
Bordagary, Bowling Green State University Center for
Popular Culture, Ammie & Paul Busby,
Tam Carlson, Janet Ferguson, Doug Fiely,
Mike & Becki Garland, Danny Gillespie, Bill Glover,
Nick Glover, Mike Greenburg, Jerry Holthouse,
Eric Jaffe, Mark Jendrek, Lisa Kaichen &
Leon Broussard, Max Kiser, Anne Krueger &
Tony Corapi, Vince Lombardi, David Neuman,
Bill Schurk, Dave Southard, Clarence Spalding,
Mark Stueve, Margaret Tang, Scott Widmeyer

Nashville Cats
Bob Bernstein, Jim Caden, Scott Chambers,
Noam Chomsky, Bruce Dobie, Townes Duncan, Liz
Garrigan, Vince Gill, Karen Hayes, Tom Ingram, Charles
Marshall, Jill Melton, Paul Polycarpu,
Jeff Puckett, Joe Smith, Tom Truitt, Jerry Waters,
Patrick Widen

Bureau of Family Affairs
Big Nana
Joseph & Mary Schaefer
Lucille Messuri; Joe & Debbie Schaefer;
Brad & Katie Pierce (JR, Mattie, Vinny, Wallace);
J.J. & Maura Schaefer (Marin, Joseph Benedict);
Matt Schaefer & Julie DiBiasio;
Terry & Katie Schaefer (Connor, Lucas);
Bob & Penny DiBiasio, Erik Holmquist &
Nancy Scott Holmquist, Tom Fahey & Patti Schaefer,
John Fahey, Tony Fahey

They Made It All Possible
Diane Arbus, St. Augustine, Richard Avedon,
Fabien Baron, Sam Beckett, Harold Bloom,
Neal Boulton, Stan "The Men" Brakhage and Kubrick,
Henri "The Hammer" Cartier-Bresson, Jim Brown,
Ty Cobb, Charles Conlan, Dino, Desi & Billy,
Karl Theodore Dreyer, Billy Eggleston, Evergreen
Review, Maria Falconetti, Bobby Frank, "Stagger" Lee
Friedlander, William Gaines, Ghoulardi,
Jim Luc Goddard, Eva Hesse, Job, Julia of Norwich,
Andre Kertesz, Bernie Kosar, Thomas Merton,
Yasujirō Ozu, Camille Paglia, David Pecker, Ramparts,
Robert Rauschenberg, John Szarkowski,
Dylan Thomas, Bruce Weber, H.G. Wells,
"Werewolf" by the Frantics, Garry Winogrand

The Family Way
Jessie Gubbins, Mike Gubbins, Lucy Gubbins
Alex Holiday, Kasey Bryan, Mohammed Mukhtar
Sammy

Final Benediction
Gerald Robert Moore

HOT